MENTORING NOVICE TEACHERS

SECOND EDITION

*This book is dedicated to my husband, Jon, and
my children, Angela, Matt, and Laura, who bring joy to my life.
I thank them for their love, inspiration, and support.*

MENTORING NOVICE TEACHERS

FOSTERING A DIALOGUE PROCESS

Debra Eckerman Pitton

SECOND EDITION

CORWIN PRESS
A SAGE Publications Company
Thousand Oaks, California

For information:

Corwin Press
A Sage Publications Company
2455 Teller Road
Thousand Oaks, California 91320
E-mail: order@corwinpress.com

Sage Publications Ltd.
1 Oliver's Yard
55 City Road
London EC1Y 1SP
United Kingdom

Sage Publications India Pvt. Ltd.
B-42, Panchsheel Enclave
Post Box 4109
New Delhi 110 017 India

Printed in the United States of America.

Library of Congress Cataloging-in-Publication Data

Pitton, Debra Eckerman.
Mentoring novice teachers: fostering a dialogue
process / Debra Eckerman Pitton.— 2nd ed.
    p. cm.
Includes bibliographical references and index.
ISBN 1-4129-3670-5 (cloth) — ISBN 1-4129-3671-3 (pbk.)
    1. Mentoring in education. 2. First year teachers. I. Title.
LB1731.4.P57 2006
370.71′55—dc22

                                                    2005032724

This book is printed on acid-free paper.

06   07   08   09   10   11   9   8   7   6   5   4   3   2   1

Acquisitions Editor:	Cathy Hernandez
Editorial Assistant:	Charline Wu
Project Editor:	Tracy Alpern
Copy Editor:	Tom Lacey
Proofreader:	Richard Moore
Typesetter:	C&M Digitals (P) Ltd.
Indexer:	Molly Hall
Cover Designer:	Michael Dubowe

Contents

Preface

Mentoring Novice Teachers focuses on engaging teachers in dialogues about what they know and on extending that knowledge so that they can support the development of novice educators. Teachers who have been in the classroom working effectively for several years have many of the skills and competencies needed to serve as mentors. Mentoring Novice Teachers builds on that knowledge, providing teachers with opportunities to expand their understanding of the mentoring process and to focus on the skills they will be using as mentors. The process of mentoring requires small talk, heart-to-heart talks, conversation, dialogue, discussion, reflection, and the sharing of ideas and resources. Mentor and mentee need to be able to speak to each other about a variety of topics in many different ways. The goal of this text is to foster a process that enhances dialogue between them. After participating in the discussions and reflections outlined in this book, the reader will have a greater awareness of what is needed to work more effectively as a mentor to a novice teacher and/or to serve as a facilitator for other teachers who are working as mentors

The second edition of this text has been modified and enhanced in response to feedback received from individuals and workshop groups who read and used this text. It provides an even stronger tool for developing mentoring skills. First of all, a reorganization and division of several chapters makes it easier to identify key concepts. This edition also expands on the practical examples and interactive processes of the first edition and includes a greater number of references to the research that underpins the text's critical concepts. More attention has been given to the mentoring of individuals with diverse backgrounds and experiences so that a helpful and supportive mentoring relationship can be established for all those involved. The rationale for particular skills is provided in greater depth, and a facilitator's guide has been added to support the use of this text in a workshop format. These changes give the reader a resource that not only provides the rationale for effective mentoring behaviors but also includes greater opportunities to practice these skills. The second edition of Mentoring Novice Teachers blends theory and practice in a format that provides practical tools to enhance mentoring skills. Conversations and dialogues which are the focus of this text are framed by the knowledge that supports each concept, creating a text that meets the needs of mentors and facilitates a means of support for novice teachers.

Acknowledgments

Upon surviving my first year of teaching high school with the help of several elementary teachers who filled the teachers' workroom with the support, ideas, friendship, and food that was so desperately needed, I learned the value of mentoring. Although they were unknowing mentors at the time, these teachers from Elkader, Iowa, listened to my complaints and offered me encouragement. They are my primary models for effective mentoring. At the time, the teachers' lounge was too smoke-filled for my taste, so I frequented the closer elementary wing of our schools' joint facilities. When I am conducting workshops for mentors or working with future teachers, I am sometimes asked about my first year of teaching, and the names of Arlene and Susan Kuehl top the list of that supportive group of teachers and staff.

Other mentors advanced my development as I moved through stages of learning about teaching. Collectively, they have provided examples of various styles of mentoring—all of them unique and all effective. Experiencing them has contributed to my understanding of the importance of effective mentoring and heightened my desire to help others serve as effective mentors. I believe that the lives of students are greatly enhanced when their teachers feel supported and have someone to help them continue to learn.

My mentors include the following individuals:

Vince Williams, who was first and who served as my cooperating teacher at Hempstead High School in Dubuque, Iowa. Vince modeled for me a powerful work ethic and a dedication to students that I have tried to emulate. He also gave me the freedom and support to develop my own teaching style.

Harriet Naden, an English teacher from Maine Township High School in Des Plaines, Illinois, who took me to my first educational conference—a powerful learning experience that I did not know existed until then.

Bob Seei, the former principal at Wilson Middle School in Plano, Texas, who mentored me in the art of conflict resolution. When I banged on his office door, seething from some injustice I felt had been perpetrated on a student or a fellow teacher, he always told me that he would gather the facts and get back to me. I wanted immediate answers, but his style modeled for me the effectiveness of waiting to make a decision until the whole picture was in sight. His answers and decisions were usually on target, even if I had to wait to get them!

Doug Warring, Sally Hunter, and Trudi Taylor from the University of St. Thomas in St. Paul, Minnesota, who mentored me during my first experience in higher education and who continue to inspire me when we confer about issues. Their caring response to my needs as a 1st-year faculty member identified for me the necessity of mentoring for all beginning teachers, no matter what level.

Bob Monson, the former superintendent of District 197 in West St. Paul, Minnesota, who was the ultimate mentor. His belief in my abilities and his encouragement gave me the strength to do a job I was not sure I could handle. His support and expertise enabled me to learn more about myself, as well as curriculum development and educational communities, and to grow and change in ways that I had never imagined.

Finally, Mike Miller, former education chair at Gustavus Adolphus College in St. Peter, Minnesota, who served as my mentor when I returned to college life and during the writing of the first edition of this text. His inclusive style allowed the department and the college to participate in decisions and learn from our collaborative work.

The cumulative effect of these mentoring experiences is reflected in my teaching and in my work style. I recognize and appreciate the challenges mentors face each day. My goal with this text is to create a knowledge base and suggest learning experiences for future mentors so they can, in turn, provide beginning teachers with the support and encouragement they need to meet the needs of their students.

Corwin Press gratefully acknowledges the contributions of the following reviewers:

Carol A. Bartell, Dean, College of Education and Integrative Studies
California State Polytechnic University, Pomona, CA

Jodee Brentlinger, Director, Personnel Services
Capistrano Unified School District, San Juan Capistrano, CA

Dolores M. Gribouski, Principal
Columbus Park School, Holden, MA

Sandra R. Hurley, Associate Vice Provost
The University of Texas at El Paso, El Paso, TX

Joe Novak, Principal
Mill Valley High School, Shawnee, KS

Hal Portner, Educational Consultant
Florence, MA

Joy Rose, Retired Principal
Westerville South High School, Westerville, OH

Barry Sweeny, President
Best Practices Resources, Inc., Wheaton, IL

About the Author

 **Debra Eckerman Pitton** began her career in education as a language arts teacher, first as a high school then as a middle-level teacher of English, speech, and theater. Over the years she has worked at various schools in Iowa, Illinois, and Texas. She has served as an Assistant Superintendent for Curriculum and Learning and as an elected member of her local school board. She has taught interpersonal and group communication at the community college level and currently is an Associate Professor of Education at Gustavus Adolphus College in St. Peter, Minnesota, where she teaches middle school methods and secondary methods and supervises student teachers.

She received her PhD in Curriculum and Instruction from the University of North Texas and has authored two books, *Stories of Student Teaching* and *Mentoring the Novice Teacher*, as well as numerous articles. She conducts mentor training workshops for school districts across the country and presents at national educational conferences. Most recently she completed a yearlong fellowship with the Minnesota Educational Policy Fellowship Program.

1

Defining the Mentoring Relationship

WHAT IS A MENTOR? ■

Today, the word *mentor* pops up in many conversations. Famous athletes speak of their coaches as mentors. Business leaders talk about mentoring a newly hired person in the operations of a company (Barrett, 2000). High schools and colleges often place students in apprenticeships with a mentor who is doing the job they hope to have some day. All of these descriptions are appropriate and are based on a trusting relationship between two people.

The term comes from Homer. In the *Odyssey*, Mentor, a wise and learned man, was given the task of educating the son of Odysseus. Mentoring is an intentional pairing of an inexperienced person with an experienced partner to guide and nurture his or her development. The goal for mentor-teachers is not to create clones of themselves but to help their mentees develop into the best teachers they can be. A mentor serves as a guide, a supporter, a friend, an advocate, and a role model (Chapel, 2003; Tatum et al., 1999).

WHY WE NEED MENTORS ■

School districts often require that novice teachers attend training sessions, expecting immediate implementation of a new idea or concept from participation in a workshop or a class. Professional development, however, does not happen that quickly, and teachers must practice, evaluate, and adjust new skills before applying them in the classroom. As with any new learning, the opportunity to hear different perspectives, reflect, and rethink is the key to true understanding. Research has shown that when educators have the opportunity to share their teaching experiences or their approaches to new ideas with other teachers, what they have learned in the training moves beyond a mechanical approach and becomes an embedded, effortless skill (Evertson & Smithey, 2000; Fideler & Haselkorn, 1999). As teachers converse about their efforts to use a new idea, an integrated, personalized approach emerges as they make connections between what they already know and do and the idea they are introducing. Reflective, systematic thinking about teaching and learning helps novices become problem solvers who can monitor and adjust their teaching to support their students' learning (Feiman-Nemser, 2003; Gilbert, 2005). Talking to other teachers, hearing differing ideas, and reflecting on their own approaches are vital to educators' continued learning and to putting any skill into practice (Schon, 1990).

The success of new teachers is critically linked to their first teaching experiences and the opportunities they are given to talk through issues they face in the classroom. Linda Darling-Hammond (2003) has identified the first year as the time that often determines whether a person will stay in teaching. The initial experience also shapes what methods and strategies the person will use (Evertson & Smithey, 2000; Storms, Wing, Jinks, Banks, & Cavazos, 2000). Those who successfully complete the first year of teaching usually do so because they have connected with another teacher. Gold (1992) developed a process for providing psychological support for beginning teachers and mentors. Her work suggests that "before any assistance can be accepted by the beginning teacher . . . a relationship must be developed between the two individuals" (Gold, p. 30). First-year teachers will often identify a critical friend whom they turn to for support in the classroom and whom they view as a role model. Wise educational leaders will identify and train mentors in practices that foster this support rather than leave this critical component to chance (Hicks, Glasgow, & McNary, 2004).

Educators have also identified the cooperating teacher as the most influential individual in a student teaching program (Pitton, 1994). Since interactions with the cooperating teacher will definitely shape the preservice teacher's future, cooperating teachers need to develop and implement the same practices used by mentors of 1st-year teachers.

■ WHY WE NEED MENTOR TRAINING

Teaching is one of the few professions that require newly trained individuals to be given immediate and full responsibility; novice teachers are accountable for the learning that does or does not occur in their classrooms. Practicing teaching in the abstract, without students, does not provide novices with the context they need to develop and hone their skills. That is why, before being licensed, student teachers must demonstrate their competence. Because novices are expected to be accountable for student learning in the same way that experienced teachers are, many states have enacted a probationary status for 1st-year teachers, along with testing and provisions for support. These programs and licensing requirements ensure that beginning teachers continue to learn and grow as they interact with students and the school community (Portner, 2005).

Student teaching and the first year of teaching are critical for supporting a novice's learning. Many scholars have written about the need to support beginning teachers in order to retain them and enhance their knowledge and skills (Cobb, Stephens, & Watson, 2001; Fideler & Haselkorn, 1999; Hobson, 2002; Johnson, Berg, & Donaldson, 2003; Moir, Gless, & Baron, 1999; Odell & Huling, 2000). Although mentoring is a key method for providing this help, individuals who assume the task of supporting developing teachers through the mentoring process are themselves not given enough direction or guidance (Giebelhaus & Bowman, 2000; National Commission on Teaching and America's Future, 2000).

A mentor is a guide for novice teachers' journey through their first classroom experience. As mentors move into this new role, their training is critical for success. The learning process for mentor development needs to involve more than just knowledge acquisition; mentors need a range of skills to be effective. Garvey and Alred (2000) state that experiential learning is one of the most effective processes for mentor training. They suggest that because mentoring is a social interaction; learning to be a mentor needs to take place within a social learning context. Active learning, focused on dialogue and conversation, therefore is a necessary and powerful tool that should be the basis for effective mentor training.

WHY BE A MENTOR? ■

Supportive, nonjudgmental relationships greatly benefit new teachers (Darling-Hammond, 2003; Evertson & Smithey, 2000). Many newly hired teachers often find themselves overwhelmed by the demands of a new job and isolated in a classroom with little time to talk to their colleagues. They may wonder if they are doing things "the right way," and they may feel frustrated when lessons and assignments do not work out as they had planned. Novice teachers often struggle as they work to apply their knowledge in the ever-changing world of their classroom, and many leave the teaching profession after their first year, frustrated and discouraged. The multiple tasks of adjusting to a new environment, dealing with the varying needs of their students, and developing their own confidence while preparing for daily lessons and schoolwide expectations can overwhelm beginning teachers. A number of researchers (Gilbert, 2005; Gold, 1992; Hicks, Glasgow, & McNary, 2004; Stansbury & Zimmerman, 2000) suggest that novice teachers need support to develop coping skills so they can handle these demands and develop self-reliance. Since 22 percent of all new teachers leave teaching within the first three years (U.S. Department of Education, 1999), it is vital that professional educators develop the capabilities to support beginning teachers (Ingersoll & Kralik, 2004). New teachers who get the support they need to develop stronger skills can positively impact hundreds of children in a district. When they leave, the school system must go through the process of finding and developing yet another new teacher, and children lose another potential advocate. By working with student teachers or 1st-year faculty members, mentors can help strengthen the teaching profession and minimize the number of new teachers who leave the classroom for other kinds of work.

Mentoring benefits experienced teachers as well. They often find that assisting other teachers with their careers and goals develops their own potential and brings about a new level of job satisfaction. The mentor's professional growth is enhanced through the collaborative focus of a mentoring relationship (Moir & Bloom, 2003). In effective mentoring, the mentor and the mentee take time to talk together about educational issues, and these intellectual interactions, based on the context of teaching, are vital to the continued development of both teachers (Brock & Grady, 2005; Wolfe, 1992). Thus, a mentoring relationship provides experienced teachers with an opportunity to expand their own learning and to use their teaching expertise in a new way.

■ A PERSONAL VISION OF TEACHING

Hayes (1999) points out the importance of a mentor's willingness to take on this role and suggests that before experienced teachers consider becoming mentors they need to fully understand what this work entails. Mentors need to know how to use their personal vision of teaching in mentoring, how to support and aid novice teachers, and what is expected of them as mentors. Reflection on these issues can help them provide the best support possible.

There are as many different styles of teaching as there are teachers, and it is important that mentors find a way to describe their personal view of the profession to begin a dialogue with their mentees. When mentors define their vision of teaching explicitly, it becomes easier for them to articulate their educational perspectives and philosophies (Garvey & Alred, 2000). Participants in the mentoring relationship can then come to a shared understanding of what teaching is all about. Having such a dialogue allows mentors to more readily assist novice teachers as they develop their own teaching style.

A simple yet powerful way to describe teaching is through the use of metaphor (Marshall, 1990). By using a literary device to synthesize their view of their work, teachers can visualize their approach to the classroom and share it with others. For example, one high school teacher uses the metaphor of an orchestra conductor to illustrate her vision of what she does. This metaphor represents her need to direct the learning of many different groups. Each group of players or students plays from the same score, but they all play different parts. When all of the parts are added together, they create a whole, beautiful, musical piece. This teacher works to meet the needs of a variety of learners while striving to help them all be successful. Thus, the metaphor of an orchestra conductor works well as a descriptor of her teaching and helps her articulate her vision of teaching.

Metaphors provide opportunities for mentors to begin sharing their visions of teaching without preaching or lecturing. The following activity can help mentors determine their vision of teaching through a metaphor that can later be shared with a mentee.

Dialogue: A Metaphor for Teaching

1. Compare the experienced teacher's metaphor of a conductor with the following two metaphors given by beginning teachers:

   A. "I see teaching as mountain climbing. As the teacher, I lead the climbers. I struggle to move up the mountain of learning step by step; and after I have made it, I turn and grasp the hands of my students, pulling them up behind me."

   B. "As the teacher, I am like a big fountain showering my students with all they need to know to be successful in my class."

   What does each metaphor say about the beginning teacher? What insights might each description give you about each novice teacher if you were his or her mentor?

2. Develop a metaphor for your own teaching. Brainstorm about the various aspects of your work and take notice of what images come to mind when you think about teaching. Avoid using examples you have heard and develop one that identifies a unique vision of your own teaching.

Once mentors have developed their metaphor, they can extend their personal vision of teaching by sharing the metaphor with a colleague and refining it to meet their vision. Mentors can use Figure 1.1 to clarify their metaphor.

Before sharing their metaphors, mentors should ask mentees to write their own. They can engage in the activity in Figure 1.2 together to begin developing a shared understanding of each other's view of teaching. Mentors who lack a mentor partner can write their answers to these questions and come back to them at a later time to reflect on their answers.

The sharing exercise in Figure 1.2 provides mentors with a process that enables them to define their own vision of teaching as well as to come to a shared understanding of individual visions of teaching with their mentees. The sharing of this understanding is an important first step in the

Figure 1.1   Developing a Personal Metaphor for Teaching

Mentor: State your metaphor for teaching and describe what the metaphor says about your vision of teaching.

Colleague mentor: State your understanding of your fellow mentor's metaphor.

Mentor: Clarify any misunderstandings or misinterpretations of the metaphor by rewording it.

Now reverse roles so both participants have the opportunity to explain and clarify their metaphor.

Figure 1.2   Metaphor Chart   .

Directions: Make a copy of this chart so each person has one to use. Complete each step, following the directions provided.

STEP ONE

Mentee:

Describe your metaphor for teaching. (i.e., "Teaching is . . ." or "Teaching is like . . .")*

_____

_____

_____

Exchange this with your mentor.

Mentor:

Describe your metaphor for teaching. (i.e., "Teaching is . . ." or "Teaching is like . . .")*

_____

_____

_____

Exchange this with your mentee.

STEP TWO

Mentee:

Describe what your mentor's metaphor tells you about his or her view of teaching. Write your description below.

_____

_____

_____

Exchange this with your mentor.

Mentor:

Describe what your mentee's metaphor tells you about his or her view of teaching. Write your description below.

_____

_____

_____

Exchange this with your mentee.

STEP THREE

Mentee:

Add to your description or clarify it if you feel that your mentor's understanding is incomplete or inaccurate.

_____

_____

_____

Exchange this with your mentor.

Mentor:

Add to your description or clarify it if you feel that your mentee's understanding is incomplete or inaccurate.

_____

_____

_____

Exchange this with your mentee.

STEP FOUR

Mentor and mentee:

A. Discuss how your revised metaphor reflects your vision of teaching.

B. Answer these questions:

   What is unique about each perspective?

   What is similar?

   How might your unique visions of teaching influence your work together?

_____

_____

*This process applies to developing either metaphors or similes.

mentoring relationship. Without such a dialogue, mentors might view what is going on in their mentees' classrooms only through their own vision. Dialogue about personal views on teaching enables novice teachers to have an opportunity to compare their own vision of teaching with a seasoned teacher's, thus helping them gain insight and perspective. Likewise, it is important that mentors understand their mentees' visions and how they influence their classroom practices and interactions. With this understanding, mentors can support the kind of learning that helps the mentee achieve that vision. Mentors also can help foster a new understanding of what teaching should be.

Unless mentors and mentees are both very clear on how they view teaching and learning, miscommunication and misunderstanding can occur. Though she might not share it, the mentor should remember that the mentee's view is his or her reality and must be considered in all conversations about teaching. Mentors can provide another way for beginning teachers to see teaching by modeling classroom interactions that demonstrate how their visions differ. Then they can ask the novice to reflect on how he or she views the mentor's methods. Through this modeling-reflection process, a novice educator's vision can be shaped to reflect new understanding of the development of teaching and learning.

After the partnership has been in place for a while, mentors should reintroduce the metaphor chart (Figure 1.2) and ask their mentees to make any necessary changes to the description of their metaphors. A good time to do this is either at the midpoint of student teaching or at the end of the semester for 1st-year teachers. This is an opportunity to discuss how mentees are working to actualize the metaphors they created. If they want to rewrite their metaphors at this point, mentors can discuss how mentees might focus their learning to support their visions of teaching. If they modify their original metaphors in a negative way, possibly reflecting frustration or stress, it is important that mentors address those underlying stresses so novices do not base their vision of teaching solely on limited experiences. Mentors can help reaffirm original metaphors or develop new metaphors that reflect newly discovered, but positive, visions of teaching.

Mentors themselves may adjust their own visions of teaching after working with a novice. Gilles and Wilson (2004) have written about mentor-teachers who described the profound effect their novice teachers had on their own teaching. Signals should be checked now and then to make sure each other's perspective is understood. If a vision is renewed or rewritten, the steps that can be taken to support this vision of teaching should be discussed.

ROLES IN MENTORING ■

Mentoring as a concept varies from one school district to the next. No matter the district, however, it is important that all individuals involved in mentoring know and understand their roles. Lack of clarity regarding mentoring roles can lead to confusion and ineffective support for novice teachers (Brooks, 2000; Chapel, 2003). Whether the process of support is for a student teacher or a 1st-year teacher, the roles of mentors, mentees, and supervisors comprise the integral triad of the mentoring relationship and must be clearly defined.

To develop mentoring skills, it is important that mentors be given the opportunity to collaborate with other mentors (Garvey & Alred, 2000). The dialogue and reflection components of mentor development need to be provided—either through a formal process or by a group of mentors-to-be who are working together to enhance their skills. To that end, it is highly beneficial if educators working on their mentoring skills find another teacher with whom to share and reflect.

The Project on the Next Generation of Teachers (Johnson, 2004) identified the concerns and issues that determine the success of a novice educator. It is important that mentors fully understand the needs, the areas of concern, and the mind-sets of their mentees before beginning mentoring relationships with them. This is not that difficult, since all veteran teachers were once novices themselves. The dialogue on page 9 allows mentors to recall that experience and to hear the experiences of others in order to better understand their mentees.

By examining roles in their mentoring relationships, as well as potential stressful moments and their own early experiences, mentors can identify situations that might arise and brainstorm positive ways to handle them.

Role Descriptions

The relationship that develops between mentor and mentee is vital to the effectiveness of their work together. When all parties know what is expected of them, the mentorship develops into an effective and supportive process (Stanulis, Fallona, & Pearson, 2002). The following role descriptions clarify the roles of each person in the mentoring relationship.

The Mentee

The role of the mentee is to be open to the process, to commit to the relationship, and to continue learning.

Novice teachers benefit from interaction with and support from someone who has been successful teaching in the classroom (Allen, Cobb, & Danger, 2003; Ingersoll & Kralik, 2004; Johnson, 2004; Johnson, Berg, & Donaldson, 2003). Thus, it is imperative that mentees be open to the idea of receiving input. Although this may seem like a minor point, if mentees believe that they have the necessary skills to be successful in the classroom, they may feel uncomfortable or even threatened by the idea of a process that provides them with support. Many people believe that they need to do it on their own for their success to be real. Some approach their first teaching experience with the belief that it is a sign of weakness or failure to accept help. They must be open to the suggestions and support of their mentors and must view their role as that of a partner with the mentor in strengthening the teaching profession. This is easier for some than for others, but it is critical that mentees recognize this aspect of their role. Mentors can help by discussing the mentee's perception of the process and acknowledging that it is often hard for people to admit they need help. If mentees can identify their concerns about the idea of mentorship, they open the door to the process. Novice teachers who do not feel they need any help and thus do not value the mentoring relationship can be a

Dialogue: Remembering Experiences

Look over the following questions and think about your answers. Share your experiences with another teacher or other mentors and listen to their experiences.

To Start the Conversation

Think back to when you were beginning your teaching career and found yourself in a new classroom on the first day of student teaching.

- What did you expect your classroom-cooperating teacher to do for you?
- How did your cooperating teacher fulfill that role?
- What did your college supervisor do to support you during that time?
- What did you do to make the experience successful?

Then, try to recall your first day as a classroom teacher.

- What kind of support did the district offer you as a newly hired teacher?
- Did you have the opportunity to talk with colleagues before you started?
- Did you find someone with whom you could share your concerns as the school year progressed?
- Did you feel isolated?
- Did you consider quitting?
- If you did consider quitting, what kept you going so that you persevered to become the teacher you are today?

To Extend the Conversation

After you have shared your beginning teaching experiences and listened to the experiences of others in your group, think about how each of the members of the student teaching triad played a role in the outcome of your student teaching experience and answer the questions below. Share your answers with a colleague.

- What might have been different if the mentor had approached his or her role differently?
- What might have been different if the supervisor had approached his or her role differently?
- What might have been different if you, as the mentee, had approached your role differently?

Think about your first job in a school district and try to remember what might have made those first days and weeks less stressful. Try to recall an actual event that was problematic for you during those first days and weeks. Visualize this event and assess the support that was offered. Then, share your answers with a colleague.

- Do you remember how you handled the problematic event?
- Do you think you might have responded differently if you had been able to talk about your ideas and plans with another teacher?
- Did anyone offer you advice that you felt was not helpful?
- Did your principal or another administrator provide you with help?
- If so, how did this feel to you as a beginner?

challenge to mentors who will need to continue to seek informal opportunities to spend time with them. By focusing on developing a comfortable relationship, mentors create situations for developing a deeper exchange.

Beginning teachers also must be willing to commit to the time it takes to work with someone else. Since many pressures and expectations are placed on them, they often consider it easier to work alone than to carve out a few minutes to meet with someone on a regular basis. Mentees' commitment to the process—their willingness to join in all of the mentoring activities and to spend time with their mentors—is a necessary aspect of a positive relationship (Tatum et al., 1999).

It is also important that the mentee sees his or her role as that of a learner. Becoming a successful teacher is an ongoing process. Most college preparation programs focus on the concept of lifelong learning, and this idea should be internalized. Knowledge brought to the mentor-mentee relationship must be used as a basis for discussion. It is important that mentor teachers stress that new understandings do not devalue what has been learned but rather extend knowledge in new directions to help meet the needs of students. If mentees see themselves as lifelong learners, they will be able to weigh new ideas and consider how these ideas fit with their own teaching philosophies. They will conduct action research to find answers to their questions. They will stretch themselves in new directions. Those who want only to perfect the tools they bring to the classroom and not venture in any new directions do not fulfill their role in the mentoring relationship (Maynard, 2000).

The Mentor

The role of the mentor is that of guide, supporter, friend, advocate, and role model.

As a guide, the mentor needs to help the novice teacher negotiate the challenges of the first year in the classroom, whether the beginner is new to teaching or just to a particular setting. Like Socrates, mentors need to provide ideas and encouragement to broaden the repertoire of new teachers so they do more than just survive, but actually extend their skills (Smith, 2005).

In the role of supporter, mentors champion their mentee's development by being accepting and always willing to seek ways to assist, despite differing views or challenging situations. They must resist the desire to create a teacher "like themselves" (Cowne & Little, 1999). Valuing differences and supporting mentees as they learn to develop their own skills and talents are critical aspects of the mentor role.

Mentors do not engage in direct instruction with a novice teacher or make specific demands. They do not impose their knowledge and skills but rather help mentees view things from different perspectives. Mentors do not evaluate novice teachers. If they are asked to evaluate or direct behavior, they are no longer serving as a mentor. A friend, a guide, a supporter, or an advocate cannot provide unbiased information to a superior. If mentors are asked to step into the role of evaluator, the relationship will be irrevocably altered. The evaluation process must be totally separate from the mentoring relationship. Confidentiality must also be ensured, and supervisors need to refrain from questioning mentors about a novice teacher's performance (Feiman-Nemser, 2001).

The stress of student teaching or of being a 1st-year teacher can be overwhelming. However, mentors and mentees accept each other the way they are and work through the difficult times, just as in any friendship. Mentors support new teachers by offering ideas and suggestions or lending sympathetic ears as mentees struggle with the complexities of teaching. A nonjudgmental, accepting approach creates a supportive environment that helps mentees manage stress. This professional friendship, which provides unconditional emotional support and understanding for the roller coaster of emotions that novice teachers experience during their initial teaching experience, is an important component of mentoring. (Tatum et al., 1999).

Complex issues and challenges can add to the stress of the first year of teaching. When mentees exercise poor judgment or are questioned by parents or administrators about the quality of their work, mentors may need to step into the role of advocate (Renard, 2003). As advocates, they may be the only people who can speak knowledgeably on behalf of a new teacher, and this may be a difficult and uncomfortable role. But if they have developed a good relationship mentors often feel compelled to step in.

It is most important that mentors also be role models. In all learning situations, hearing about how to do something is never as effective as watching it being done. As Tatum et al. (1999) point out, novice teachers watch everything their mentors do. As most school cultures are quite complex, it is imperative that mentors model the types of behaviors and interactions that are expected. Respect for peers, a student-centered focus, and a collaborative approach to teaching and learning are just a few of these behaviors. Mentors who lead conversations about effective teaching strategies and professionalism but fail to exhibit these qualities themselves are not providing their protégés with complete mentoring.

Above all, mentoring is a social relationship (Garvey & Alred, 2000). Mentors need to be willing to spend time with their mentees so that they can get to know one another. The value of the mentoring process depends on the strength of this relationship.

The Administrative Supervisor/College Supervisor

The role of the supervisor is primarily that of evaluator, although he or she may also serve as an advocate and a supporter.

A principal or a college supervisor has the duty of assigning a grade or writing an evaluation for the novice teacher. The supervisors' observations are tempered by their obligation to document the effectiveness of the beginning teacher for purposes of licensure, continued employment, or tenure. These decisions make it imperative that supervisors not be privy to all of the tribulations of mentees.

The supervisor's role often requires a more direct approach than the mentor's supportive role. Although some supervisors can temper their observations, suggestions, and comments with an air of support, the very nature of their role as an evaluator can create angst for mentees (Feiman-Nemser, Carver, Schwille, & Yusko, 1999). However, supervisors can be of great help to mentors when a mentee is failing to heed comments and guidance. A supervisor's comments can add weight and importance to a mentor's previously discounted suggestions. If mentees are not attempting to incorporate suggestions from their mentors, supervisors can point out these same issues to heighten awareness. This may be an unplanned occurrence, or mentors may solicit a supervisor's help in focusing the novice on areas where more learning is needed.

Supervisors may also be able to stand up for mentees when questions about their performance arise. Supervisors carry more influence than mentors; if they see potential and effort in a mentee, they can communicate effectively and with authority to those questioning his or her skills. Supervisors may not prefer this role, but it is an option. In taking it on, they can shield beginning educators from undue outside scrutiny that might weaken their progress.

Flexibility of Roles

The roles of supervisor and mentor may be reversed in some cases. During student teaching, the classroom teacher may become more of an evaluator than a mentor, making directive statements to the beginner and offering little emotional support. This shift may occur when the classroom teacher is asked to grade the student teacher (Hobson, 2002). If the mentor or cooperating teacher has evaluative power, the relationship will be adversely affected. In these cases, the college supervisor or school administrator may need to take on the role of mentor to provide an empathetic ear for the mentee.

At other times, the college supervisor, in addition to the classroom teacher, may take on the role of mentor. This creates an extremely supportive environment, but at some point the quality of the student teacher's work needs to be discussed. The college supervisor or the classroom teacher then needs to shift roles to evaluate; when he does so, it is important that he clearly identifies his role as evaluator at that time, so the mentee is aware of the focus of the conversation.

Roles in mentorships are usually more clearly established with 1st-year teachers than with student teachers. A principal who serves as the administrative supervisor and who evaluates all beginning teachers should not ask the mentor for evaluative information. Although principals are interested in the development of beginning teachers and may ask general questions about how things are going, mentors and supervisors should never exchange information about evaluation.

The key to fostering a positive mentoring process is communicating and understanding roles and role expectations (Geen, Bassett, & Douglas, 1999). Mentors can use the prioritizing checklists in Figures 1.3, 1.4, and 1.5 to develop a shared understanding of roles in their mentoring triad. These checklists can serve as starting points for a discussion of what mentors and mentees expect from the relationship. They were compiled by experienced mentors from various school districts and reflect the activities that correspond to each role. Each participant in the mentoring relationship should fill out the checklists for all roles, then discuss with the others in the triad why he or she considers an item to be a valid expectation for each role. In this way, perceptions about the roles and responsibilities for all participants in the mentoring experience can be identified and discussed. Participants should explain their priority rankings to each other to clarify their personal vision of the mentoring process. This type of dialogue clearly defines the roles and expectations of everyone involved and helps create a strong start to the mentoring experience.

Dialogue: Mentoring Roles

- Complete the following checklists (Figures 1.3–1.5) on the mentoring experience on your own before using them with your mentee. Then compare your responses with a colleague—either other teachers who are developing their mentoring skills or a fellow mentor. Are your priorities for mentoring similar or different from your colleagues? How does your vision of these roles impact your approach to the task of mentoring? (If you are working independently, it is important to consider other perspectives and think about how an alternative view would impact a mentoring relationship.) Give yourself sufficient time to reflect on these expectations and identify your level of concern for each item. When you are comfortable with using the checklists, after having reviewed them with a colleague, you can use them with your mentee.

- After all participants in the mentoring relationship (mentee, mentor, and supervisor) have completed all of the forms, share your answers with each other. Discuss any variances in fellow participants' ratings. Address any major differences or misunderstandings. Discuss why particular components of the roles may matter more to one individual than another. Discuss how each individual can adapt and/or compromise his or her vision of these roles to reflect the needs of the others in the triad.

- Although you may find that you want to add items to these lists or move expectations from one list to another based on your particular program, please use the list as it is or create new site-based lists so that all members of your mentoring group have the same items to prioritize and discuss. Be sure to rank each item according to your own values. There is no right answer; this is simply a way to capture ideas about expectations from each member of the triad so these views can be explored in future dialogues.

Figure 1.3   Expectations for the Mentee

The following list identifies the expectations for mentees.

Please prioritize the list by giving each item only one number. Give a score of 1 to the most important expectation, of 2 to the next most important expectation, and so on, through 22.

The mentee will

_____ come to the student-teaching semester/first year of teaching exhibiting enthusiasm, a love for learning, and a genuine liking for young people

_____ be open to developing a relationship with the mentor

_____ be willing to try new ideas and suggestions offered by the mentor

_____ bring to the experience ideas for topics and subjects that he or she would like to incorporate in his or her teaching

_____ bring to the experience a solid knowledge base, including an awareness of district, state, and national standards

_____ bring to the experience a willingness to work hard

_____ get to know the facilities, personnel, environment, and political structure of the school

_____ be willing to create an interactive classroom via discussion groups, cooperative learning lessons, and by engaging students in higher-order questions, projects, and activities

_____ develop lesson plans that reflect varying formats

_____ develop and articulate a classroom management plan

_____ develop flexible lesson plans that can change when schedules and student needs dictate

_____ develop lesson plans that break down a concept and create a process for teaching it

_____ identify objectives for the day and lesson (on the board, verbally, or in lesson plan) and share objectives with students

_____ implement a variety of assessment strategies

_____ commit to teach a unit that he or she develops without relying on a text

_____ identify his or her own learning style and explore how this learning style impacts his or her teaching

_____ observe teachers from a variety of subject areas and varying grade levels

_____ plan lessons that engage students of varying degrees of ability

_____ get involved in the total school experience, via extracurricular activities and all teacher duties, meetings, etc.

_____ communicate with the mentor-teacher daily

_____ exhibit a strong presence—the ability to communicate positively and professionally in the classroom

_____ address the various learning styles and multicultural identities of his or her students

Figure 1.4   Expectations for the Mentor-Teacher

The following list identifies expectations for mentor-teachers. Please prioritize the list by giving each item only one number. Give a score of 1 to the most important expectation, of 2 to the next most important expectation, and so on, through 30.

The mentor-teacher will

_____ communicate his or her expectations and objectives for the student teacher/1st-year teacher at the start of the mentoring relationship

_____ allow the mentee to develop his or her own teaching style

_____ (for student teachers) assist the mentee in developing a schedule that identifies the gradual induction process (i.e., one class one week, adding a class and prep on a weekly basis; or two classes of the same prep that can be repeated later in the day, allowing for the mentor-teacher to model a class that will be taught by the student teacher)

_____ review the mentee's management plan and inform the mentee of school and district discipline policies

_____ provide information about the school and district

_____ arrange for release time to team-teach with the mentee early in the semester or year

_____ arrange for introductions to other staff members, administrators, and school personnel

_____ maintain confidentiality

_____ arrange and encourage observations in other classes, levels of ability, and grade levels

_____ arrange for the principal to observe the mentee in a nonevaluative mode

_____ arrange for social interactions with the mentee

_____ identify his or her own learning style and discuss with the mentee how this style impacts his or her teaching

_____ provide an opportunity for the mentee to videotape his or her teaching both early and late in the semester or year

_____ encourage the mentee to implement a variety of curricular, teaching, and assessment strategies

(Continued)

Figure 1.4 (Continued)

_____ model infusion of multiculturalism on a daily basis (beyond the curriculum, as a part of life in the school)

_____ model instruction that is differentiated for students with varying needs

_____ create a schedule than ensures communication with the mentee on a *daily* basis

_____ model effective interpersonal communication skills (in parent conferences, with administration and other faculty, and with students)

_____ talk with the mentee about career paths; discuss his or her goals and plans for the future

_____ discuss the legal issues of education with the mentee

_____ provide the mentee with information on state requirements and mandates and describe processes in place for meeting these expectations in the classroom

_____ be aware of what is going on in the mentee's classroom by observing on a regular basis

_____ provide evidence of the mentee's classroom interactions and teaching strategies to the mentee following observations

_____ review lesson plans for alignment with standards (check written plan and/or have mentee rehearse, discuss, or visualize)

_____ provide the mentee with the opportunity to develop and teach his or her own curricular materials

_____ review the observational tool (the lens) that will be used

_____ offer suggestions in areas requested by the mentee

_____ share curricular materials

_____ confer with the supervisor as needed

_____ serve as advocate when issues or concerns become problematic

Figure 1.5   Expectations for the Supervisor

The following list identifies expectations for the supervisor in the mentoring relationship. Please prioritize the list by giving each item only one number. Give a score of 1 to the most important expectation, of 2 to the next most important expectation, and so on, through 15.

The school administrator or the college or university supervisor will

_____ provide regular contact and observation of the mentee during the student-teaching experience or first year of teaching

_____ communicate with the classroom teacher on a regular basis (without seeking evaluative information)

_____ assist the mentee in addressing future goals and career paths

_____ provide seminars during the mentoring experience to discuss relevant issues and provide time for reflection

_____ require all student teachers to attend the fall or spring workshop at the site where they will be student teaching

_____ make sure 1st-year teachers and student teachers are aware of state and district mandates and requirements

_____ expect a broad range of instructional strategies to be implemented and provide staff development/coursework to support this expectation

_____ expect a broad range of curricular activities and assessment strategies to be implemented and provide staff development/coursework to support this expectation

_____ provide and encourage a selection process in which mentor-teachers are chosen according to their qualifications to serve as master teachers

_____ communicate expectations to the mentor-teacher and the mentee

_____ address the legal issues associated with teaching prior to the mentee's work in the classroom

_____ refrain from using the mentoring process as a means of gathering evaluative information

_____ implement a mentoring program that provides support for the mentor (in the areas of time, resources, and training)

_____ serve as advocate for the novice teacher when others question the methods or processes they are using

_____ when evaluating, provide opportunities for the mentees to discuss observations before forming opinions and generating conclusions about their teaching

2

The Heart of Mentoring

Trust and Open Communication

Mentoring is relational. And, as in any relationship, interactions between mentors and mentees must be based on trust (Hicks, Glasgow, & McNary, 2004; Roberts, 2000). Without trust, it is difficult to be sure of another person's motives and, as a result, both mentors and mentees may approach conversations warily. Trust is vital to achieving the goal of the mentoring relationship—which is to support novice teachers and assist with their continued growth and development.

BUILDING TRUST ■

It is easy for someone to say "Trust me," but the words must be backed up by actions and other statements that prove the trust is warranted. When novice teachers are assigned a mentor—someone they have yet to know personally—trust is not yet established. The desire to trust may be there, but trust is not automatic; it takes time to develop. It is imperative that mentors take time to build trust with their mentees at the start of their relationship (Bouquillon, Sosik, & Lee, 2005). Although the first days of a novice educator's teaching experience are very hectic—leaving them without much time to spend with their mentors—mentoring programs should schedule meetings in order to start the trust-building process. Educators who are considering serving as mentors but who are uncomfortable with the necessary time commitment, should reconsider their plans (Brooks, 2000). Mentoring is often like parenting. Parents are never sure how much time and effort will be needed to support their children, but they are committed to doing whatever it takes to help them be successful. Mentors must be similarly committed to giving their time and energy.

Once mentors have determined that they are comfortable with the time commitment required for this role, they need to use their initial interactions with the novice teacher to build their relationship. From the very first meeting, they must show themselves to be available and empathetic (Rippon & Martin, 2002). One way to do this is to share ideas and experiences. Without sharing, there is no relationship. Mentors and mentees can begin by meeting for coffee, going to lunch, or attending a mentor/mentee breakfast or afterschool seminar prior to any in-depth conversation or classroom observation. Talking about experiences, hobbies, and leisure activities allows mentors and mentees to get to know each other.

The first steps in a relationship require some self-disclosure. Mentors who share information about themselves usually find that their level of intimacy is reciprocated. Dindia (2000), Metts (2000), and Rosenfeld (1979) found that if one shares information about oneself, the listener usually responds. Individuals often refrain from self-disclosure because they are afraid they might project an image they do not want to present. Trust develops when one takes a risk and discloses a thought or feeling, and the other person responds in kind. When sharing stories and information becomes more comfortable and natural, mentees are able to trust their mentors more as they share their own fears and concerns. Mentors should reveal their personal sentiments while keeping in mind an appropriate level of self-disclosure. Without such disclosure by mentors, it is unlikely that mentees will feel they can share their feelings or concerns. Reciprocal sharing, starting with safe topics and building up to more difficult issues, is the path to building trust.

The challenges of building trust and mentoring effectively are magnified in cross-cultural mentorings (Johnson-Bailey & Cervero, 2004). Stereotypes may influence perceptions of behavior and communication style when educators who bring with them very different background experiences work together (Thomas, 2001). Mentors need to consider that their behaviors may be overlaid with issues of power, historical tensions, and institutional racism. To enhance mentoring in cross-cultural situations, it is imperative that ongoing discussions about race and racism between mentors and mentees be honest and open.

Self-disclosure can be especially challenging when individuals are unsure that their story will be accepted. When sharing an experience that is radically different from that of the mentor, mentees need to be heard and to have their experience validated. Discounting or ignoring the influence of these life stories can prevent the development of any type of supportive relationship.

Mentors can use metaphors to describe their visions of teaching (as outlined in Chapter 1) and to structure initial discussions once they get beyond introductory conversations. It is also helpful for mentors to initiate a discussion on the roles of mentees, mentors, and supervisors (see Figures 1.3, 1.4, and 1.5 in Chapter 1). Discussing metaphors and roles allows for the development of a shared vision of teaching and of expectations for the mentoring relationship. It is very important that mentors not assign any negative value to a mentee's vision of teaching or to the way he or she assesses mentoring roles. Instead, mentors can discuss similarities and differences in perspectives to identify what is held in common. A trusting relationship makes discussing differing perspectives easier, and being aware of the other person's perspective gives the relationship a starting point to build on.

Mentors should read the conversation on page 22 to get a sense of how they might work to build trust. They can then analyze it for tips on how to approach initial conversations and write out some ideas for their own initial conversation with their mentee. Practicing and reflecting on dialogues can help mentors feel comfortable creating trust-building conversations (Rippon & Martin, 2002).

After sharing thoughts with a partner or writing down ideas, mentors can see if their thoughts were similar to those of other mentors-in-training who responded to this exercise. Mentor-teachers who have reviewed this dialogue identified comments that are welcoming (Did you find your way okay? Would you like some coffee?); self-disclosing (I get lost. It doesn't seem that long ago that I was a beginning teacher); empathetic (It can be hard finding your way around here); that share feelings (I remember the way I felt when I started teaching); and that build rapport (Where are you from? How did you decide to become a teacher?). All of these comments, statements, and questions are designed to start building a trusting relationship.

Mentors can use other questions and comments as conversation starters, such as the following:

- What do you like to do on the weekends? Do you play golf, tennis, etc.? (Suggest other faculty they might be able to connect with who also play a sport.)
- Have you been to the new mall? There are lots of great restaurants over there.
- Did you get to travel much in college? I really want to go to _____.

Mentors can also share some of their own experiences in the initial conversation, such as the most difficult situation they experienced while student teaching and the most challenging aspect of their first year of teaching.

To avoid initial conversations that take on the tone of an interview—or, worse, an interrogation—mentors can lead in using a connection to their own lives. For example, a mentor might preface the question about leisure time by saying, "I really enjoyed this summer [or the weekend, or a holiday]. I was able to do _____, which I really enjoy. What do you like to do when you have nothing on the calendar?"

Prefacing statements in this way allows the conversation to flow more naturally. If mentors reveal something about themselves before asking a question, they create a personal connection with the new teacher.

OPEN COMMUNICATION ▪■

Open communication is necessary to build trust, and trust is necessary for open communication. The existence of this loop makes it difficult for

SCENARIO

Scenario for Trust Building: Initial Disclosure

Role-play and analyze this initial conversation on your own or with another mentor. While reading this sample dialogue, look for signs of trust building, and think about what else you notice in the mentor's choice of conversation.

Mentor: *[shakes hand with mentee]* Hi, _____! Did you find your way to the school OK? *[Mentee shakes his or her head.]* Oh, sorry to hear that. Would you like some coffee or a soft drink?

Mentee: Thanks. I'd love some coffee . . . finding my way here took a little longer than I had expected.

Mentor: Well, it can be hard finding places around here. When I go anywhere new, I always have to allow extra time for getting lost!

Mentee: I'm just not used to judging how long it will take to get places driving in the city.

Mentor: Well, that will get easier. I'm just glad you're here so that we can chat a little and get to know each other a bit. So, this is your first teaching job?

Mentee: Yes, I graduated in June.

Mentor: Well, your first teaching position is a big deal and you should feel good about being hired to work here—we had a lot of applicants.

Mentee: The interview process was tough, that's for sure.

Mentor: Well, it doesn't seem that long ago that I was starting my first year of teaching. I know a lot has changed since then, and it will be fun to hear ideas on teaching from someone who's fresh out of college! I still remember how I felt when I started teaching—kind of scared, but excited, too.

Mentee: Yeah, it feels a little overwhelming.

Mentor: Well, we'll take care of that soon enough. So . . . fill me in. . . . Where are you moving from? Do you have a place to live here yet?

Mentee: Well, I'm from north . . . a little town not too far from the state college. I haven't started moving, but I've got a lead on an apartment not too far from here.

Mentor: Great! Well, I am looking forward to having someone to work with, _____. I have always loved teaching. . . . Tell me, what led you to a teaching career?

Mentee: Oh, I really like working with kids. I spent a lot of time babysitting and working at camps when I was younger, and I'm always amazed by the things kids can do. I had some wonderful teachers myself, and teaching seemed like such a positive thing to do with my life.

Mentor: That is so true. Well, are you ready to check out your classroom?

Mentee: Sure!

Debrief with a partner regarding the conversation or write down your thoughts about these questions.

- What did you hear in this initial conversation?
- How did the mentor begin to establish a trusting relationship?
- What would you talk about next?
- Did you hear any examples of self-disclosure? If so, describe the example and identify how it was/was not matched by the listener.

Figure 2.1   Ground Rules

Rules and processes apply to both parties.

The following are the ground rules for conversations between _____ (name of mentor) and _____ (name of mentee).

We agree to the following:

1. Confidentiality and honesty. We will say what we are thinking and feeling when we talk to each other, knowing that everything we say will be held in strict confidence.

2. Ask questions. If we are not sure about what has been said, we will ask, "What do you mean?" We will avoid filling in the blanks with our own interpretation—we will check signals and ask for clarification.

3. Create and stick to a schedule. We acknowledge that regular, planned times for conversation, observation, and informal get-togethers are vital to developing our relationship. If we have trouble connecting, we will set up a time for a phone call or conference to discuss the issue, and we will follow up on all concerns in a timely fashion.

4. Respect each other's needs and communication style. We will share our perspectives on communication needs and style, and respect one another's views. For example, it is okay to say that the timing of an unplanned conversation is not the best or that we are uncomfortable with some aspect of a discussion.

5. Others???? _____

Signed by: _____ (name of mentor) and _____ (name of mentee) Date: _____

mentors to know where to begin their focus. It is important that they remember that this process is not linear, but circular, and so a starting point is needed. Mentors can establish trust more easily while working to communicate openly if some ground rules are established for interactions (Garvey & Alred, 2000). While the term *ground rules* may sound negative and perhaps unnecessary, communication conflicts can be avoided with a plan for approaching conversations. Mentors can use the guidelines in Figure 2.1 for their ground rules or create their own to fit the needs of their relationship. These ground rules can be a starting point for developing trust and open communication.

Ground rules state publicly what both partners agree to do within the context of the mentoring relationship. The commitment to these rules provides a solid base from which trust can be developed and open communication can occur. One expectation that should be included in all ground rules is confidentiality (Feiman-Nemser, 2001). Without an initial agreement that all comments, observations, and discussions are confidential, the relationship cannot develop. Trust will evolve more quickly if a commitment is made regarding the privacy of conversations.

During the getting-acquainted process, and particularly in a cross-cultural relationship, it is critical that both parties talk about how they communicate and include any diverse communication perspectives in their ground rules. For example, during an initial conversation, mentors should identify their personal preferences for communication and ask mentees to share their preferences. A mentor might say, "I really find that I like to think about an issue for a while before I am ready to decide what to do about a problem. I know that some of my colleagues like to jump right in with solutions, but I like to mull things over. So, I may be very quiet about things while I am thinking. This doesn't mean that I am not happy about what I have observed or what we are discussing, it just means I am thinking. I wanted you to know that so you can get a sense of my communication style. What about you? How do you like to approach issues?"

Mentors need to self-evaluate and describe their own communication style honestly. For example, if they react with intense emotions, speak loudly and authoritatively, or dislike spending a lot of time hashing over issues, they should make this style clear and, most important, invite the novice teacher to share his or her preferences for communication. Because mentees may use or prefer a different communication style, mentors need to set up ground rules to identify and validate both. Mentors, because of their greater level of experience and training, need to take the lead in establishing this pattern of honest and open discussion about communication.

Mentors should also keep in mind that certain patterns of communication have been described as gender-related. For example, Deborah Tannehill (1989) states that when men respond to a problem, they often include specific ideas for solving the issue, while women lean more toward nurturing and empathic statements. These communication behaviors also need to be explored by the mentor and mentee to determine if they reflect their styles (Cuddapah, 2002).

Open communication is based on honesty and trust and takes into consideration the use of verbal, nonverbal, and paralinguistic interactions. Mentees sense that their mentors are truthful from their words (verbal), their physical expressions and body language (nonverbal), and the tone and inflection of their voice (paralinguistic) (Manusov, 2005). Messages are sent when individuals communicate, but the meaning of those messages is perceived only in the mind of the individual who hears them. While no mentor intentionally sends mixed signals, if insufficient attention is paid to the use of verbal, nonverbal, and paralinguistic messages, miscommunication results (Lindley, 2003).

Verbal Messages

Verbal messages are often considered to be the most reliable part of a dialogue. How can spoken words be misinterpreted? Individuals cannot be sure that the verbal messages they send actually are heard by the listener (Dindia, 2000). A wife, for example, often checks signals sent by her husband on the amount of gas left in their car before using it. If she hears him say, "There is enough gas to get you there," she believes she has at least a quarter of a tank. If, after hearing this from her husband many times, she has consistently found the needle on the gas gauge to be near empty, she may feel that her husband is not giving her a straight answer. According to his view, however, he is telling her the truth. He believes that even if the gas gauge is near empty, there is enough gas to get her to most places she wants to go. She does not have the same understanding of how much gas is "enough." Over time, this couple has come to understand that "there is enough gas in the car" can mean one thing to her and another to him. Yet, their awareness of the difference in meanings has enabled them to prevent conflict. Individuals in any relationship need to carefully check signals to be sure that what is said has a similar meaning for both of them.

Mentors can read the following conversation to analyze the impact of verbal signals in communication.

Scenario: Focus On a Verbal Message

SCENARIO

Ask two people to read the following exchange between a novice teacher and a mentor while you listen. After you have heard the exchange, list the ways that the verbal message (*words only*) could be interpreted.

Mentor: Hi, Sam. I found it really interesting observing you in class today. I'm glad we can take some time to discuss what went on.

Mentee: Yeah, things didn't go exactly as I had planned.

Mentor: Let's talk about that. What did you plan and how did the actual lesson vary from that plan?

Mentee: My goal was to have the kids explore the various properties of paper by having them feel the paper, write on it, tear it, and soak it in water—and I had a whole bunch of different types of paper for them to use. I had wax paper, construction paper, cardboard, typing paper, notebook paper, toilet paper, and paper towels.

Mentor: There was a lot for them to explore.

Mentee: Yeah—maybe too much. They were so busy doing the tearing and soaking that they didn't write down any of their discoveries.

Mentor: I didn't hear any of the directions you gave the students.

Mentee: Well, it was a discovery lesson.

Mentor: Discovery? Hmmmm.

Mentee: We learned about teaching by discovery in my methods class at the university.

Mentor: Do you think that this particular "discovery" lesson accomplished what you were trying to do?

Debrief with a colleague or write out your answers. What are the various ways that the words used by the mentor could be misinterpreted? What about the word choices of the mentee? Try rewriting this dialogue using different word choices to see if you can find some clearer language. Ask two people to read the dialogue again, so you can practice listening to your word choices and their possible implications.

Some mentors who analyzed this conversation came up with these suggestions for clarifying the verbal message:

- Using the word *interesting* to describe the lesson might be interpreted negatively by the mentee. A simple "Thanks for letting me hang out in your class today" might be a better beginning, as it does not allow for misinterpretation.
- The question "What did you plan?" is supportive because it suggests that the mentee actually did have a plan.

- The reaction "Discovery? Hmmmm" might be interpreted as a negative comment through which the mentor indicates this is not something he or she cares for, or it might be interpreted as inquisitive. In either case, the word choice is open to misinterpretation by the mentee.
- The mentee's statement, "Well, it was a discovery lesson," might seem to be justifying his or her decision.

This role-play demonstrates that mentors need to think about their word choices to make sure they are not being misconstrued. For example, to clarify the meaning after saying "interesting," the mentor might have said, "I am always amazed by all the various methods that can be used in the classroom." This kind of explanation can help avoid misinterpretation.

Avoiding Misunderstandings

There is no way for individuals to be absolutely sure that what they say is interpreted exactly as intended. Therefore, it is important that mentors check signals by asking questions when they are not sure about what they have heard, and it is equally important that they are sure their words are heard the way they intended. If mentors think they might have heard something incorrectly, they need to ask, "So you are saying that. . .?" or "Do you mean. . .?" to check the accuracy of their interpretation (Johnson & Johnson, 2002). Without checking signals, mentors may have a false impression of what occurred in the classroom or an inaccurate view of what mentees think. If the relationship has a solid foundation based on trust, it is easier for mentors to ask if their mentees are comfortable with the communication that took place and be sure they have received an honest answer.

Another way mentors can avoid misinterpretation is to give the lead in a conversation to their mentees. For example, when first talking about a classroom observation, mentors should not immediately qualify what they have seen. They can say, "Thanks for giving me the opportunity to see students in action," or "I appreciate you letting me spend time in your class." Mentees are usually eager to know if mentors liked a lesson or not; thus, initial comments may be interpreted as approval or disapproval. A mentor's lead-in statement should not indicate feelings. Lead-in statements should be nonjudgmental and emotionally neutral, so mentors do not inadvertently send a signal that interferes with the discussion that follows. If mentees think their mentor did not like their lesson, they may become defensive and unable to hear comments and suggestions. On the other hand, if mentees think their mentor liked the lesson, they may discount suggestions for improvement. Statements such as "That was interesting," "That was nice," or "Wow, I'd be worn out after that class" are vague and can be misinterpreted by an anxious beginner. It is easy to imagine a novice teacher thinking, "An 'interesting' class? What does that mean? Was it too rowdy? Is she saying 'interesting' because she doesn't want to be critical? Was it 'interesting' because there was so much going on that needs to be fixed?" A neutral lead-in serves as a transition from the lesson to the conversation about the lesson.

As mentors and mentees work at open communication, ground rules are useful tools for mentors to refer to as they check for clarity. If ground

Dialogue: Exact Language

Ask another mentor or mentee (or even a family member or a friend) to list what they mean when they say the following statements and then answer the questions yourself. Next, share your interpretations with each other. What did you learn about yourself and the person you exchanged lists with regarding your understanding of the words? How can you use this knowledge in your work with your mentee?

What do you mean when you say or ask the following (be as specific as possible)?

- "I'll be there in a few minutes."
- "Can I borrow a couple of bucks?"
- "What do you think?"
- "Come here a second."
- "I'll be right there."
- "It needs some work."
- "It's okay."
- "Lots of times."

When you use these words, what do they mean to you?

- Sometimes
- Always
- Never
- Usually
- Maybe

rules are established that indicate that both will work to be open and honest with each other and that both need to clarify if something is confusing, a reference point for checking signals is established. Mentors can work toward open communication by saying, "In our ground rules we agreed to be open with each other. So, I would really like it if you would let me know if there is anything I said that is confusing to you or that doesn't seem to connect with what you are thinking."

Mentors can further investigate the importance of checking signals through the exercise above.

This exercise demonstrates how important it is to use exact language to help avoid misinterpretation. If, for example, a mentor states that his or her mentee never gets the students refocused after a disruption, this imprecise language may create a barrier, as the mentee might think, "It's not true that I *never* get the students refocused." The mentor might have used *never* for impact or just failed to consider how it might be interpreted. "That was good," "I liked that," and "That needs some work" all use imprecise language. Mentors can prevent misinterpretation by saying specifically what was good, exactly what occurred in the classroom that they liked and why, and identifying what needs some work. Specific communication can be much more accurate and effective.

Nonverbal Messages

Many people have probably heard the statement, "It's not what you said, it's how you said it." This comment exemplifies how the nonverbal components of communication must be considered as well as the verbal. Nonverbal signals include facial expressions, vocal tone, inflection, and body stance. It is important that nonverbal messages match verbal messages, as people often tend to pay more attention to these signals than to words (Manusov, 2005; Metts, 2000). People's faces and bodies often reveal what they are feeling, even if their words do not. If someone frowns as she tells her guest that she is glad he dropped by to visit, the guest gets the message that she is really not very pleased to see him. If a person lowers his eyes and looks away as he tells a colleague that he likes her idea, she may get the message that he is not sincere. Listeners add meaning to the messages they hear as they make sense of the words and interpret nonverbal signals. Sending contradicting verbal and nonverbal signals is a common cause of miscommunication. Mentors can communicate more accurately by being aware of nonverbal messages.

Mentors also need to be aware that nonverbal communication contains culturally sensitive components: the distance people stand from each other when speaking, their eye contact, the way they take turns talking, how they listen, and when they choose to communicate. When cultural backgrounds differ, it is important that the mentor think carefully about these differences (Peterson, 2004).

Tone of voice is a component of nonverbal language called paralanguage, and it is what is remembered more than the words a speaker uses. Early research by Trager (1958) identified paralanguage as the meaning that occurs in conversations beyond or in addition to the words we speak. The match or mismatch between what is said and the tone used is very important in conversations. If the tone of voice matches the words, the message is believable; if the tone is incongruent with the words, it is the tone, not the words that delivers the message.

It is important that mentors match their tone to their verbal message. If a mentor tells her mentee that she wants to support him but uses a contradictory or inconsistent tone, it is the tone, not the words, that will be heard. For example, if a mentor tells a mentee that he likes the way she called on her students in class but says it hesitantly while looking away, the mentor sends a nonverbal cue that he does not necessarily mean what his words convey. Mentors can try the exercises on pages 29 and 30 to heighten their awareness of nonverbal communication and the use of paralanguage.

Mentors who discussed the questions following the dialogue exercises noted that it was not always easy to match their vocal tone and nonverbal signals. Yet, having an awareness of their use of tone and the ways in which they created the tone they wanted was important to them. By listening to themselves and working with peers, these mentors felt they were able to monitor their own use of tone and nonverbal signals to create accurate messages. They agreed that it was important to convey confidence, even if there was some doubt in their mind about the novice teacher's capabilities, and that the vocal tone was very important when doing so. If mentees hear mentors tell them they are improving but also hear uncertainty, they probably will not believe what is said. This leads to a lack of self-confidence and to

Dialogue: Nonverbal Practice 1

DIALOGUE

Say or ask the following to another mentor or videotape yourself. Try to convey the positive emotion listed in the parentheses. If you are using a video-tape, watch your physical stances, gestures, and facial expressions and listen to your verbal tone when you play back the video. If you are having another mentor watch you, have your partner tell you what they see in your face and body and what tone and voice they hear. Answer the questions at the end of the exercise. The goal is to get a sense of how you convey these emotions.

"I think you're doing a great job!" (enthusiasm)

"When you said that to the students, what was their response?" (thoughtfulness)

"The class was on task, even if they were a bit loud." (confidence)

"I know it's hard to find time to create your lesson plans." (support)

"Do you want me to give you some suggestions?" (questioning)

"I really enjoyed watching the students interact in their small groups yesterday." (pleased)

"It's tough when a parent gets angry with you." (empathy)

"I saw what you did with the fourth-grade math lesson on fractions yesterday." (awe)

Follow-up questions:

- From your observations or the feedback you received, describe how your nonverbal signals matched your messages.
- What might you need to do to change your tone, facial expressions, or body language to more accurately reflect the words you are speaking?

---

distrust. Mentees expect honesty, and if they get a sense that their mentor does not mean what he or she says, the relationship is hurt.

Mentors can use the dialogue exercise to identify nonverbal and paralinguistic signals that accompany negative emotions. By becoming aware of these signals, mentors can work to avoid them.

These dialogues identify the contradiction that occurs when a person says something that might seem positive but that is uttered with a negative tone and body language. When such a contradiction occurs, the listener focuses on the emotion conveyed.

It is important that mentors practice matching their tone to the words they speak, especially when conversing with a mentee. Awareness of tone, facial expression, and body language helps one match verbal and nonverbal messages. Mentors can use a mirror or practice with a friend to increase their ability to monitor their tone and nonverbal messages.

The aspects of nonverbal communication listed on page 30, which can be culturally or gender-based, should be given focused attention in all mentoring relationships (Manusov, 2005). They can influence the impact of conversation and, in turn, relationships, so it is important that mentors explore them with their mentee (Blake, 1999; Obidah & Teel, 2001; Peterson, 2004).

Dialogue: Nonverbal Practice 2

Practice saying the sentences and questions listed below using the identified negative emotion and accompanying nonverbal signals. Videotape yourself or have another mentor provide feedback. This exercise strengthens your awareness of the tone, stance, gestures, and facial expressions that accompany *negative* emotions, so you can monitor your own interactions to avoid inadvertently sending a message that you do not intend.

"I think you're doing a great job." (hesitancy)

"When you said that to the students, what was their response?" (anger)

"The class was on task, even if they were a bit loud." (sarcastic)

"I know it's hard to find time to create your lesson plans." (unbelieving)

"Do you want me to give you some suggestions?" (demanding)

"I really enjoyed watching the students interact in their small groups yesterday." (sarcastic)

"It's tough when a parent gets angry with you." (unconcerned)

"I saw what you did with the fourth-grade math lesson on fractions yesterday." (disbelief)

Follow-up questions:

- What did you pay more attention to, the words or the emotion (nonverbal message) of each sentence and question?
- How would you feel if you heard these messages (and accompanying tone)?
- What could you do to create a more positive tone/emotion to match these verbal and nonverbal messages?

Proximity

Everyone has a comfort level regarding the personal space that surrounds him or her during conversations, so standing too close to a person you are talking to can be disquieting. When a mentee may perceive the mentor as having more power (e.g., during student teaching), standing too close while talking may heighten the sense of dominance. This is not productive when trying to develop trust. If a mentor feels crowded or finds herself leaning away during conversations, she may want to identify and discuss how she and her mentee view "personal space" in conversations. Mentees may also exhibit these behaviors, and mentors need to respond when they see them. Naming the issue and sharing perspectives about proximity in conversations is the first step in creating positive communication patterns.

Turn Taking

A speaker who does not allow someone to complete what he or she is saying, jumping in with comments or suggestions, can give the impression of not caring about the other person's comments. Interrupting minimizes a speaker's contributions to the conversation. In open communication, each member of the conversation has an equal right to speak, and taking turns is important. Jumping in and cutting off conversation can inhibit the careful listening that is a part of effective communication. Conversations between mentors and mentees should not be about one person telling the other what to do—they should be about sharing ideas, experiences, and information to reach conclusions about educational practice. Identifying differences in turn-taking and working to listen carefully can minimize incorrect perceptions.

Eye Contact

There is an expectation in North American and European cultures that individuals should look each other in the eye when they converse. If the listener looks away, the speaker may perceive a lack of interest. On the other hand, when someone stares during a conversation, it can be disarming. Mentors should strive to use the appropriate level of eye contact to reflect their interest and support. Checking signals regarding the use of eye contact is important, especially if one observes behaviors that differ from one's own. Mentors should strive to identify and provide a comfortable visual connection during conversations.

Listening

There is a listening stance that communicates that someone is paying attention to what is being said in a conversation. In many cultures, a person who is leaning forward and concentrating on what the speaker is saying signals that he or she is listening. Eye contact, nodding, smiling, and other facial expressions also identify that the listener is focused on what is being said. Effective listening means asking occasional questions to ensure that the listener is on the same page as the speaker. Mentors who are good listeners also ensure there is balance in a conversation and give their mentees plenty of opportunity to talk about what is happening in their classroom. Listening does not mean offering solutions, but often is simply being there to absorb and reflect what the novice teacher is saying. Listening can be a powerful support, and mentors need to be sure that they utilize effective listening behaviors in all conversations.

Use of Time

Allowing significant time for a conversation to occur is another signal that the message is important. If mentors set up a time to talk and then frequently change the meeting time or look at their watch and seem eager to get going, mentees may feel that what they have to say is not valued. This undermines trust and prohibits open communication. Some individuals and cultures are not as time sensitive as others, and mentors and mentees need to address these differences if they occur. Discussions about the use of time and what it means to each individual to be on time can help develop a positive mentoring relationship.

BUILDING A MENTORING RELATIONSHIP WITH AN EXPERIENCED COLLEAGUE ■

Age and experience can also impact a mentoring relationship. An experienced teacher who is new to a school or district will appreciate induction

Figure 2.2   Mentor Model: Peer Dialogue and Data Gathering

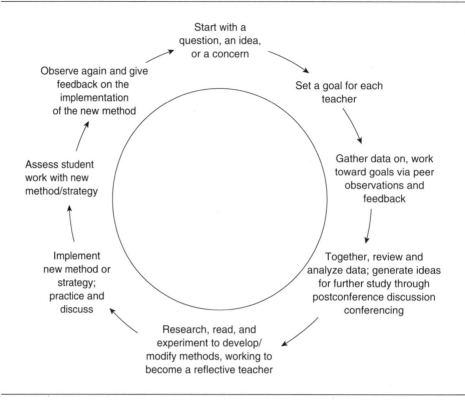

Start with a
question, an idea,
or a concern

Observe again and give
feedback on the
implementation
of the new method

Set a goal for each
teacher

Assess student
work with new
method/strategy

Gather data on, work
toward goals via peer
observations and
feedback

Implement
new method or
strategy;
practice and
discuss

Together, review and
analyze data; generate ideas
for further study through
postconference discussion
conferencing

Research, read, and
experiment to develop/
modify methods, working to
become a reflective teacher

support and information but may prefer a peer coaching model rather than the traditional mentoring approach (Little, 2005). When two colleagues work together and give equal respect to each other's expertise and experience, the potential for mutual growth is increased (Daresh, 2002). While the needs of the experienced teacher in transition to a new setting should not be overlooked, mentors need to carefully check their communication processes and language choices to maintain mutual respect when mentoring a veteran educator. Peer observations by both members of the mentor/experienced teacher relationship should be encouraged (Fabian & Simpson, 2002), and program expectations should be modified to take into account the background of the experienced teacher. The model in Figure 2.2 provides a process for peer conversations that can be used when mentoring experienced teachers.

The experienced teacher who is implementing new curricular ideas, trying new teaching methodologies, or adopting new assessment techniques in a different grade level or school setting can feel like they are back at the starting block. These experienced teachers can also benefit from the support and guidance of mentors who work with them to implement, gather feedback, and reflect on their methods and practice so they continue to improve. However, this process needs to be invitational. Any attempt to force a mentoring system onto an experienced faculty member will probably be met with resistance. Offering mentors as a support device—in the role of a peer coach, a confidential, nonevaluative guide-on-the-side to new methodologies—is a key component in effectively providing this service.

The same communication guidelines that are used with novice teachers apply to veteran educators. It is very important that mentors ensure confidentiality as well as recognize and build on the expertise of seasoned educators. It is also helpful if mentors make connections between the new methodologies and the practices veteran teachers have been using in order to validate their previous work. Many teachers can adopt the innovation for which they are receiving support more easily if they see the connection or relationship between the practices they have been using and the new concepts.

Above all, when working with veteran teachers, mentors need to be respectful of the history and years of wisdom that these educators bring to the classroom and approach the interaction using a peer-mentoring process. It takes time to change gears and do something differently, and mentors need to allow time for these veteran mentees to gradually develop their comfort level and expertise. Working with experienced teachers has an additional benefit. Mentors of veteran teachers often find the learning process to be reciprocal.

By paying attention to the process of communication, mentors can develop trust and provide for open dialogue. Even when they are of varying gender, race, age, or experience, communication can be effective when participants in the mentoring relationship acknowledge and address communication components and styles (Peterson, 2004). In doing so, they will generate greater levels of trust. Novice teachers will not share important issues or concerns if they are unsure of their mentor's response, so little will be accomplished. In order to have important discussions that lead to improved teaching and higher levels of learning for students, mentors must continually check signals to foster trust and open communication.

3

Understanding the Needs of the Novice Teacher

All beginning teachers need to focus their development on certain areas. No one starts a teaching career able to handle all situations. Accordingly, telling beginners they are performing well and then not providing them direction serves no purpose. The mentor's job is to help a novice teacher identify areas for continued growth. Dialogue with mentees is more effective if communication is open and honest (see Chapter 2). Honest communication allows the mentor to see what is happening in a classroom and to provide the mentee with specific information in a manner that enables him or her to hear the message. Obviously, this communication works best if mentees are aware of their needs and communicate them. Their comments, such as "I know I need to work on how I transition between subjects," or "I am not sure about structuring my groups for cooperative learning. Do you have some suggestions?" provide mentors with a positive starting point for discussing mentees' needs.

However, early in a relationship, as trust and open communication are just starting to develop, mentees may not yet feel safe enough to reveal their perceived weaknesses. They may be so overwhelmed that they do not know what to focus on first, or they may be unaware of some of the problems in their classrooms as they struggle to get through each day.

Student teachers are in a unique position with regard to sharing weaknesses because their prospects for employment can improve or worsen depending on the mentor/cooperating teacher's letter of recommendation. Their desire for a positive letter may make student teachers fearful of revealing their weaknesses. Although a letter of recommendation is not an evaluation, student teachers often regard it as their ticket to a job and so want to be seen by their mentors only in a positive light. Likewise, 1st-year teachers know that they are on probationary status, and this awareness can affect their willingness to discuss areas of concern. This problem is avoided when the college supervisor or principal (see Chapter 1), rather than the mentor, does the evaluating. If, for some reason, the mentor must also be the evaluator, all parties in the mentoring relationship must understand that it will be difficult for the mentee to be completely open and honest, making the relationship less productive than it might be otherwise. When mentors step into the role of evaluator, the relationship between them and the novice teacher changes. However, if trust is established and mentors use supportive language, mentees may overcome their initial concerns with this evaluation process.

Mentors must be able to identify issues their mentees might not be aware of and support them as they learn how to address these concerns. If things are going well in the classroom and there are no apparent areas of concern, mentors can help novice teachers move into new areas of learning and set realistic goals for continuing to develop their skills.

◼ DEALING WITH A RANGE OF NEEDS

Novice teachers enter the classroom with their skills at a variety of levels. Some new teachers are very well versed in various methods for engaging students in the learning, while others are comfortable with only one strategy, such as large-group instruction. Many novice teachers have limited experience in day-to-day classroom interactions and need support in developing positive learning environments and effective techniques for classroom management. No matter where they are when the relationship begins, the mentor's job is to help the mentee move forward.

Mentees may begin their teaching experience with differing levels of skills, but they all move through similar stages of development as they hone their teaching strategies. It is often helpful for mentors to consider these stages in light of the mentees' ability to see clearly what is happening in the classroom. These levels of development are described in various ways (Bouquillon, Sosik, & Lee, 2005; Head, Reiman, & Theis-Sprinthall, 1992; Moir & Bloom, 2003), but they usually proceed as follows:

• Focus on the self. Completing the day-to-day work of teaching and figuring out how to do the job is the primary focus of most mentees when they begin teaching. This stage is characterized by their concerns about how they personally are doing. Questions such as "Did I have too much of . . .?" "Did you notice how I . . .?" or "Did you like the way I . . .?" show that they see themselves as the primary focus of the classroom. At this stage, they often articulate their concerns about how they are performing and request items that address their needs: "Where do I get things copied?" "How do I take attendance?" or "What should I do about homework?" Mentors can respond to these types of questions with direct statements that allow mentees to move beyond this self-centered stage. By providing specific answers and by asking new teachers to think about how the lesson worked for the class or for a particular student, mentors can shift the mentee's focus. Novice teachers who continue to see teaching in terms of what they do as opposed to what students do need to be prompted in a more direct fashion to consider the outcomes of this perspective on student learning.

- Focus on the class. As mentees develop confidence, their focus shifts, and they start to see the needs of the class. At this point, they voice concern for their students' learning and not just for their own performance. Their comments move from a focus on self to consideration for the class as a whole. Questions like "Do you think they got it?" "Were there enough materials for all of them to do the work?" and "Will the class enjoy this book?" depict a concern for learning. When novices ask such questions, mentors need to respond with ideas and resources.

- Focus on individual students. After a while, new teachers begin to see individual students and react to their needs. Statements like "Juanita has trouble with . . .", "Mark needs to be challenged more in reading," and "Kyeesha is easily distracted and should sit by someone who will be a role model" show a growing awareness of the uniqueness of each student. This higher level of awareness identifies a teacher who has moved beyond the initial reactive and self-preservation stage and no longer sees the class as a collective body but as individuals with various learning needs.

Figure 3.1 illustrates these stages of development. When mentees reach the stage of perceiving the class as individuals with various needs, mentors should not direct the conversations but should let novices direct the problem solving (Feiman-Nemser, 2003). Listening to mentees as they plan to address student needs and offering support for their decisions facilitates their independence as educators. If they struggle with this problem-solving process, mentors might offer suggestions—in the form of questions—to direct their thinking, such as "I wonder if that will help Sarah keep focused in class?" and "Do you think that will work for all the students?" Guiding questions are always appropriate and helpful, as they allow mentors to gently redirect and focus mentees' thinking while encouraging the development of their problem-solving abilities. In addition, providing new resources, ideas, and methods will help novice teachers find answers to questions they have about their students' learning (Boreen, Johnson, Niday, & Potts, 2000).

Throughout the mentoring experience, one of the most meaningful gifts mentors can give mentees is the time and opportunity to reflect on their teaching. The ability to be reflective provides new teachers with the skills to continue their own learning long after the first years of teaching (Portner, 2003; Storms et al., 2000). By listening to their concerns, describing what is happening in the classroom, and asking guiding questions, the mentor can support the mentee's efforts to enhance his or her learning. If new teachers develop the practice of thinking carefully about what occurs in the classroom, they will find ways to continually improve their teaching and learn to meet individual student needs. Reflection enables teachers to find answers to their own questions and enhances their professional satisfaction (Schon, 1990); as a result, the students in their classrooms are more likely to flourish. Educators who never are asked or given the opportunity to reflect on their practice cannot be expected to grow and learn.

Figure 3.1   The Expanding Vision of Beginning Teachers

As they develop their expertise, novice teachers shift their vision from a focus on themselves to the class as a whole and to an awareness of the needs of the individual students who make up the class.

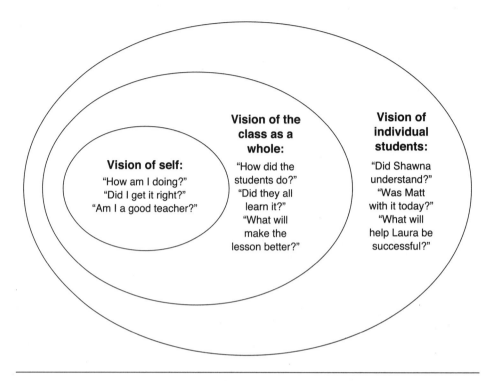

Novice teachers have many needs that mentors must support. These vary greatly in depth, but the following list identifies those experienced by all new teachers to some extent. Mentors can determine which ones to focus on by interacting with their mentees and getting to know them.

- The need for empathy and personal support
- The need to accurately see what is happening in the classroom
- The need for guiding questions
- The need for an action plan and resources
- The need for honesty

The first three will be addressed in this chapter, and the others in Chapter 4.

The Need for Empathy and Personal Support

New teachers move through several emotional states during their first year. They are anxious about starting their careers and surviving the rapid pace of the school year. They may feel disillusioned throughout the year when things do not go as well as they had envisioned. Then, they reach a state of rejuvenation as they move into the final months of the first year, and as they develop strategies for even more success in the future and begin to anticipate the next year (Bleach, 1999; Moir & Stobbe, 1995). Student teachers pass through similar stages in a more compressed time frame.

Mentors need to acknowledge the very real emotions their mentees experience. Empathy—the ability to relate to another person's emotional state—is extremely important (Stansbury & Zimmerman, 2000). Frustration, anxiety, exhaustion, and even fear may surface as novice teachers struggle to balance their personal lives with their new careers. Mentees may even become upset that they are experiencing these emotions. Mentors must give mentees permission to feel their emotions and not suppress them while maintaining a balance and being careful that their feelings of empathy do not obscure their view of their mentees' work. Too much empathy can inhibit a mentor's ability to help a mentee identify and work on areas of concern.

Empathy can be best communicated through listening. Beginning teachers should be able to communicate concerns and honest emotional reactions with mentors they trust. They must be allowed to express their feelings without fear of being thought of as someone unable to handle the job. At times, a mentor's silence and sympathetic ear is the only support a mentee needs.

The wide range of emotions novice teachers experience during their first months in a classroom requires attention be given to their emotional and physical health, as well as to their academic development (Young, Bullough, Draper, Smith, & Erickson, 2005). They need someone to provide them with personal support as they cope with the ups and downs of their initial experience. Mentors need to act as sounding boards for new teachers, comforting them and reflecting the emotions they express. Although often the listening and reassurance mentors provide may be enough, at other times guiding questions may be needed to help the mentee problem-solve ways to deal with their emotions. For example, if mentees talk about how frustrating it is to get students to move from one activity to another, mentors can ask them if they want to work on their transitions, and this can be the first step in an action plan dealing with transitions. Emotional outpouring is often the beginning of recognizing a need for change, and mentors can offer support just by listening.

Mentors also may need to give their mentees permission to let go of some things or to reprioritize their life and work. In their drive to be successful, some novice teachers fail to take care of their personal lives or their health. Observant mentors listen for signs that their mentees are not making time for life outside the classroom. Mentors can encourage mentees to maintain hobbies, exercise, and relationships that provide the emotional balance that is key and which mentees need in order to devote sufficient time and energy to the classroom.

Mentors have several options to help address a mentee's emotional needs. They can bring in another mentor for observation and conferences with the novice teacher. A mentee can more readily hear cautions about keeping life balanced when more than one mentor is voicing the same concerns. Mentors should also find ways to connect the mentee with other novice teachers who are at the same point in their careers. A study group or seminar can be a way of allowing them to share their experiences and learn from one another. This can be done within each school, or mentors within a district can bring all their mentees together. Providing opportunities for sharing feelings about the fears, frustration, and fatigue that usually accompany an initial teaching experience is especially important for mentors who find that being empathetic is not a natural emotional response. These opportunities can be given at a seminar, where novice teachers can learn from, share with, and provide support for each other.

The role-play on the next page demonstrates dialoguing with a mentee who is experiencing emotional stress. It serves as an example of how mentors can provide emotional support.

Mentors can use support statements as a starting point for conversation if they are unsure of what to say when a mentee is at an emotional impasse. The statements and questions listed in Figure 3.2 provide mentees with validation and affirmation of the emotions they are feeling, thus allowing them to recognize their needs and develop plans to satisfy them. The support statements and questions acknowledge the difficulties of the job and help mentees identify ways they can alleviate their stress.

Figure 3.2   Support Statements and Questions for Responding to Emotions

You can do it, you just need more time.

Everyone develops his or her skills at a different pace.

All learners, including teacher-learners, learn in different ways.

What do you think your strengths are?

What are you doing to release your tensions and stress?

Trying new methods is scary, but you will get more comfortable with _____ (a method) as you use it more.

Taking risks is never easy, but I will help you.

Change is hard.

You seem to be feeling _____ (an emotion). Is that right?

What do you think is causing you to feel _____ (an emotion)?

What are you doing to keep yourself healthy during this often stressful time?

The Need to Accurately See What Is Happening in the Classroom

In the early stages of teaching, many mentees are unable to see the big picture. They are often unaware of how (or if) students are learning and may not notice much of what is going on in their classroom because they are so focused on their own actions as the teacher. This limited vision inhibits their ability to reflect on interactions that create positive learning experiences. When mentees are still learning how to become comfortable with the role of teacher, mentors need to reflect back to mentees what they see during their observation. Providing a description of what is going on during a lesson without qualifying it or judging it as right or wrong is important (Feiman-Nemser, 2003).

Initially, mentors must provide a mirror, an accurate image of the classroom. A video camera provides an exact image, but sometimes when viewing a tape mentees can see only themselves and their own actions and

Scenario: Providing Emotional Support

Your mentee has been fighting a cold for several weeks and has been out sick for a few days. When she returns, her energy level is still low. She expresses frustration at the amount of time it takes her to plan and prepare for her lessons, which cuts into the sleep and rest she knows would help her get, and stay, healthy. Write out your ideas about what you might say to her before you read the dialogue below.

Mentor: So you were out sick for a few days, I hear.

Mentee: Yeah, I had that flu that's going around. I usually never get sick. I can't believe that this is the second time in two months that I've had to stay home!

Mentor: It's really hard to think about school and stay on top of lessons when you don't feel well. Teaching is hard enough to do when you're feeling 100 percent! Do you think there's any reason why you've been sick more recently?

Mentee: Well, I can't help but feel that the students bring in all of their germs and share them with me! And I have to admit I feel sort of stressed out at times.

Mentor: Like I said, teaching is hard work—both emotionally and physically. It's hard to avoid getting sick when you feel run down. Are you taking vitamins and getting enough rest so you can fight off all those germs you encounter?

Mentee: How can I ever get enough rest when it takes so long to plan for all my lessons?

Mentor: It is easy to get run down when you have the stress of a new work experience as well as cold and flu season to contend with. I know it's hard, but you need to carve out some time for yourself, so you can stay healthy. What do you do for relaxation or to unwind?

Mentee: Well, I used to go to the health club a lot, but I haven't gotten there in months.

Mentor: What did you used to do there?

Mentee: I liked to use the weight machines and do a little jogging around the track.

Mentor: That sounds like just the thing to get rid of any stress and keep your energy level up. What if you planned to take 45 minutes on your way home from school each night to stop in and get in a quick workout?

Mentee: I feel like I have so much to do.

Mentor: But you get less done when you get sick and have to miss days of school.

Mentee: Yeah, I suppose you're right. I could make a little time, I guess. I just need to write it in my schedule book, along with all the other stuff I have to do!

Mentor: That would be great. It's important to find balance in your life. You'll enjoy your students and have more energy to plan and engage in the learning when you feel healthy.

Dialogue: Emotional Support

After reading or hearing the dialogue on page 41, review what you wrote or thought, indicating how you would respond to the mentee. Discuss with a colleague or write down how your own ideas were similar or different from the example. Then, role-play your own ideas with a colleague or another partner to practice using language that is emotionally supportive.

not the responses of the students or interactions within the classroom. In addition, new teachers may feel overwhelmed after seeing what is happening in the classroom on tape. The mentor can share this information more comfortably by reiterating what happened in the classroom and sharing this feedback with the novice teacher (Rippon & Martin, 2002). Accurate descriptions of the events, conversations, and behaviors observed in a classroom, done without judgment or praise, are powerful supports for learning. New teachers may not be aware of all that is going on in their classrooms. A written description lets them see their interactions more closely. Specific methods for reflecting what is seen in the classroom are given in Chapter 7, but initial, informal conversations about observations are a good starting point. The scenario on page 43 gives mentors practice presenting neutral classroom observations. Take a moment to read "Mirroring a Classroom."

Feedback for the scenario, such as "You should have explained brainstorming before passing out the assignment," "This would work better," or "I always do it this way," does not allow novice teachers to see what is happening in the classroom. These types of comments are more direct and indicate that a mentor is doing more than just mirroring what happened. Mentors also should be careful not to overwhelm their mentee by listing every area of concern from an observation. Mentors should select one area, such as the teacher's use of language in the dialogue above, and identify the actual statements used by the teacher to share. For example, the mentor might say, "I heard you say to the students that what they were going to do was easy, and another time you told them that 'they are not babies and should be able to get into groups without so much noise.'" The mentee may respond with an explanation of why something happened or an idea about what he or she might need to do in the future. However, in the initial stages of teacher development, mentors may need to be more directive. Following up a reflected statement (such as the one in the example above) with a question, such as "What do you think about that?" enables mentors to avoid making judgments about what they heard and prompts reflection. If mentees do not recognize areas where they need to be working, mentors need to use "I messages." "I noticed that Carlie was drawing pictures during your explanation, and I wonder what you might do to address this" is an example of a direct statement that is not accusatory because it focuses on the observer's perspective. Even with direct statements, mentors should use language that will not create defensiveness, and I messages can help (Johnson & Johnson, 2002).

Once mentees have reflected on their areas of development, mentors need to offer them some resources. Recommending a book about the area

Scenario: Mirroring a Classroom

SCENARIO

Review the following scenario, or role-play it with a colleague. When you are finished, use the questions following the role-play to give another mentor or a colleague a description of what you saw in a nonjudgmental way (using effective verbal and nonverbal skills as identified in Chapter 2). If you are working alone, write down your thoughts or use a tape recorder to capture your comments. Reread or listen to them after you have completed the task. Work at mirroring what you saw and avoid making any qualifying remarks.

Setting: Eighth-grade middle school language arts classroom

Teacher: Okay, kids, we finished reading *The Outsiders* yesterday, so now I want you to get into groups and brainstorm ideas so you can write an essay on the theme. So why don't you find three other people and get into your groups. *[Students begin pulling chairs across the room and calling out to friends to form groups. Some sit alone and look around. The teacher picks up a stack of papers.]*

Teacher: While you are getting yourselves together, I will hand out the form I want you to complete as you brainstorm. It's really easy, but all of you need to contribute to the group to get it done. Okay, okay, get in your groups now. Somebody needs to get together with Sammy, he's all by himself over there. *[Teacher walks to the still-forming groups and hands out a form to every student.]*

Student: Do we all need to fill this out?

Teacher: Yes, but you need to work together. *[To the class]* You will all need a brainstorming sheet to do the essay. Hey, quiet down—you're not babies and you should be able to get into groups without so much noise, for crying out loud! *[Students finalize their groups and Sammy pulls his desk to the side of a group of three other students. A student raises her hand.]*

Teacher: Yes, Shondra?

Shondra: I don't get what you mean by brainstorming.

Teacher: It's just a list of ideas that could be the focus of your writing. You have to have a thesis, you know, and this is a way to capture all of your ideas so you can narrow down your choices and determine the one that you want to write about. Remember that the theme is what the author is trying to tell us in the book, the message. This form gives you a list of the characters and key events in the book to use as a springboard for your ideas—so get busy.

of concern or suggesting that the novice teacher visit a teacher who is skilled in the area being discussed provides the novice teacher with a way to gather information. Finally, mentors need to ask about plans for addressing the issue being addressed. Accessing resources is the first of

Dialogue: Observation

What did you hear in the scenario you read or heard? How would you mirror this teaching event for the teacher without qualifying or judging what occurred? Answer the following questions to practice reflecting events.

When watching your class, I saw . . .

When observing your class, I heard . . .

Now share your comments with a colleague and discuss the differences between your statements.

several specific steps that must be taken to improve in the area of concern. This process should be used on one or two concerns at a time. When mentors mirror all the negative things they see, their mentees can become overwhelmed, rendering the mirroring ineffective.

Mentors also need to mirror the positive things they see. In the scenario above, for example, the mentor might say, "I saw that you were using cooperative learning and had structured the activity with a set of directions for the students to use." All reflections need to include images of strength as well as areas of concern. Novice teachers cannot tackle four or five separate issues at a time. Mentors should focus on the most obvious or crucial issues and then balance the reflection by identifying what went well in the lesson.

Mentors may use the observation note form in Figure 3.3 as a tool to gather information during early observations. It provides statements and questions to foster reflection following an observation.

The Need for Guiding Questions

After mentors provide mentees with a description of what is happening in the classroom, it is hoped that they will recognize the need for some action or change. At this point they may ask specifically for help and guidance. Observations and questions that indicate that they realize they must shift the focus to the students include "I could see that some of the students really didn't get it," "They really weren't listening to me, were they?" "How do I get them to listen to me?" and "How can I increase their ability to stay on task?" If mentees do not identify issues to address from the classroom reflection, mentors can ask guiding questions to help them consider the classroom interactions more thoughtfully: "Why do you think this happened?" "What was your goal at this point?" "What might have caused the students to respond that way?" The focus of such questions is not about telling mentees what to do but about helping them discover ways to improve their teaching and supporting their efforts to learn and grow. Although some mentees quickly move beyond the self-centered stage and begin to focus on their students, mentors need to continue to observe and reflect on what they say to their mentees to support their growth.

Figure 3.3   Observation Note Form

Complete the mentor portion of the form, then share it with your mentee. Ask the designated questions, fill in the responses, and then ask what steps can be taken to address areas of concern and maintain positive areas.

Observation Notes

Mentor: _____   Date: _____

Mentee: _____   Class/Grade: _____

When watching your class, I saw . . .
(List one positive observation.)

What do you think about that?
(Record mentee response.)

When watching your class, I saw . . .
(List one area of concern from the observation.)

What do you think about that?
(Record mentee response.)

When observing your class, I heard . . .
(List one positive statement you heard.)

What do you think about that?
(Record mentee response.)

When observing your class, I heard . . .
(List one statement you heard that might be a concern.)

What do you think about that?
(Record mentee response.)

Next Steps:

If questions do not help prompt a novice teacher's awareness of areas for growth, mentors must be more directive. By asking them to role-play the student (or parent, administrator, or whomever) involved in a problem, mentors can model a more effective response to a situation. For example, mentors can set up a role-play by asking the mentee to be the student or parent who was part of a problem. The incident is re-created, and the mentor role-plays the teacher and provides a response to the situation that reflects a more experienced and/or appropriate perspective.

This type of role-play shows mentees how they might change their behavior to match the response modeled by their mentors (Rippon & Martin, 2002). In a very direct way, it gives guidance about how to respond in a given situation. Debriefing after the role-play is important to help the mentee identify what the mentor did that created a more positive outcome. By naming the mentors' behaviors as observed in the role-play, mentees identify specific behaviors they should be using. Another option is for a mentee to role-play him- or herself in a situation where the mentor's role is that of angry parent or disruptive student (or whatever the area of concern may be), so the mentee can practice what he or she might say and do before facing the real situation. These learning tools are valuable and powerful.

Mentors can reflect on the feedback scenario on the next page, in which a mentor is taking part in a classroom observation to practice the use of guiding questions.

For some mentors, guiding questions come to mind easily. However, for others, it may take practice to let go of the need to tell mentees what to do and develop the ability to ask about what happened in a nonthreatening way (Feiman-Nemser, 2003). Mentors can use the following sample questions and statements as a starting point for helping their mentees reflect on their teaching following an observation (see Figure 3.4).

If these questions do not lead mentees to reflect upon the observation and areas for growth, mentors can move to the second level of questions (see Figure 3.5), which aim to extend thinking and reflection by focusing more on areas that may need development.

Figure 3.4   Beginning Guiding Questions (for Post-Observation Conversation)

How do you feel about today's lesson?

How do you think it went today?

Did you accomplish what you set out to do today?

What were you expecting from today's lesson?

What have you been working on?

What can I help you with?

What in today's lesson would you like to talk about?

Scenario: Observation and Guiding Questions

Read this description of a lesson, or have two colleagues role-play it, and look for areas in which you think this novice teacher can focus her growth.

Setting: Mary is teaching a track unit to her high school physical education class.

Mary: Okay, we are going to learn about how to do the high jump today.

Student: Who cares about this stuff?

Mary: If you want to go out for track or watch a friend at a track meet, you need to understand how to successfully complete the high jump. I only have one high jump station, so this half of the class can do stretching exercises from our fitness plans while this half does the jump. *[Mary divides the class, puts half of the students behind her, and tells them to practice stretches.]*

Mary: *[To the group at the bar]* So your approach is at an angle, see, and you run up to the bar slowly. This isn't about speed, but energy. As you approach, you want to give a kick up, like you would kick a soccer ball, then arch backwards over the pole. *[She demonstrates.]* We will start with the pole low and see how far you can get.

Student: I can't do that!

Mary: Sure you can. *[She lines up the other students and has them practice the jump, raising the bar each time.]*

Mary: Good job! You should go out for track, Thomas! Why don't you watch Thomas do the jump? Okay. *[Students in the jumping group watch Thomas jump, as does the other group. The stretching group sits around and talks about the weekend and plans for social activities. Mary gives individual feedback after each student jumps and helps them improve the approach, takeoff, and jump.]*

Mary: Okay, you each have gotten to jump several times; let's raise the bar now and see who can keep jumping as it gets higher. *[Speaking to the other group]* Tomorrow, you guys can go and this group will do the stretches.

Dialogue: Reflecting on Guiding Questions

Review the scenario above using the observation note form (see Figure 3.3). Identify other things you heard or saw in the lesson. After you identify what you heard or saw, determine what types of questions you would ask your mentee to guide him or her to an awareness of what was going on in the class. Write down your thoughts to reflect on later or talk with another mentor to see if you have similar thoughts and ideas.

Scenario: Feedback Conversation

Now read or role-play the actual dialogue that occurred during the feedback conversation for the class described on page 47. This conversation demonstrates the type of guiding questions a mentor might ask after observing this lesson.

Mentor: Mary, all the students in the second group were able to complete the jump as you demonstrated—that was impressive for their first time.

Mary: Yeah, I think my demonstration was pretty good. I had to practice it a lot because I never did track myself.

Mentor: I noticed that you divided the class into two groups—can you tell me about that?

Mary: Well, we were supposed to go outside where there are two stations for high jumping. I had planned to have both groups jumping at the same time. But it was raining, so we had to make do with the one station here in the gym. I wanted to do two groups at the same time, but this way I was able to really watch the one group and I gave them pretty specific feedback. I think I was able to note their errors and correct them pretty well. Like you said, all of them got over the bar at least once.

Mentor: What about the other group?

Mary: Yeah, well, they were working on their stretches, which is part of our ongoing fitness plan.

Mentor: How successful was this group in getting the stretching done?

Mary: Well, they seemed to be doing their stretches, I mean I know they would have rather been jumping too, but that just wasn't possible. Tomorrow they'll get their turn.

Mentor: Is there any other way you could organize the jumping with one station so that two groups could go?

Mary: Well, I suppose I could. It just seemed like there would be so many students all waiting in line, and I thought they might not listen to me with everybody talking and stuff.

Mentor: Do you ever have two groups do an activity and alternate—with one person from each group?

Mary: Oh, yeah I've done that with some games I've set up. I see how that would work— I didn't think about two groups because I had planned for one so I just went ahead with things basically the same way.

Mentor: How would it have worked if you had alternated with two groups?

Mary: I guess that would have kept them all involved more, and I could have given the demonstration to all of the students—now I will have to repeat the entire lesson for the second group tomorrow. I think that the group that was supposed to be stretching was not all really doing the stretches, so if I had two groups and had them do the stretches while they were waiting their turn, at least they'd all be in front of me so I could see them.

Mentor: I agree, those ideas would really strengthen your lesson. What will you do now?

Mary: Well, I guess I should give the second group their time to do the jump. But I will at least have the stretching group over in front of me so that I can watch them tomorrow. The next time we do something in groups, I will have to figure out how to alternate them and try to keep everybody involved. And I guess I should think more carefully about a plan B when I am teaching something that relies on going outdoors.

Mentor: That sounds like a good plan!

Dialogue: Guiding Questions

After you are finished reading the conversation on page 48, discuss it with another mentor, or think about your ability to identify and reflect back to a mentee the things you heard and saw in the lesson. Identify whether or not you observed issues similar to those identified by the mentor in the example. List the guiding questions you heard the mentor use, then talk about your perception of the effectiveness of these guiding questions.

If a mentee still is not aware of what occurred in the classroom during the observation or is aware of what occurred but is not sure how to change the situation, mentors can ask more direct questions, as demonstrated in the third category of questions (see Figure 3.6). These questions can help direct the conversation toward areas of growth by showing the correlation between relationships or offering suggestions regarding areas of concern.

After reading the examples in Figures 3.5 and 3.6, you may feel fairly comfortable generating guiding questions to lead the conversations. There may be times, however, when a mentor would like to direct the conversation to help the novice teacher recognize more specific aspects of his or her practice. The guiding questions/probing statements in Figure 3.7 are designed for mentors who want to promote a teacher's reflective thinking and problem solving ability. Early on in the year, the questions are usually more direct. Later, the questions are more indirect and require more input from the mentee teacher. The level of questions is based on Bloom's taxonomy, and the goal is to help beginning teachers move from the more concrete levels of learning to more abstract knowledge so they can begin to problem-solve on their own.

Figure 3.5   Questions to Extend Mentee Thinking and Reflection

Tell me more about that.

Why do you think that happened?

What does the students' work tell you?

What about the students' behavior leads you to think that?

How else might you do that?

Figure 3.6   Question/Statements to Direct Mentee Reflection More Specifically

I wonder what would happen if you tried _____ ?

What do you think would happen if you did _____ ?

Does _____ (mentee's action) relate to _____ (student behavior)?

How might _____ (mentee's action) affect _____ (student behavior)?

Figure 3.7   Helping Beginning Teachers See Their Classroom: Purposeful Guiding Questions

1. Knowledge questions—to get at the specifics of what happened.

   "Who/what/when/where/why/or how did _____ occur?"

2. Comprehension questions—to get their interpretation of events.

   T ell me about/describe/discuss/explain or summarize today's class or an event."

3. Application questions—to encourage them to relate events to knowledge.

   "How was the lesson addressing the objective (or standard)?"

   "Tell me about the choices you made in the classroom today."

4. Analysis questions—to develop their ability to reflect on the lesson.

   "Compare what happened in the first hour to what happened in the second."

   "What does the students' work tell you?"

5. Synthesis questions—to encourage them to put together knowledge and events.

   "What might happen if you asked _____ to do _____?"

   "What ideas do you have about that?"

6. Evaluation questions—to identify areas of strength and areas to work on.

   "What was the best thing that happened today? The most challenging?"

   "Describe your strengths as a teacher; identify a goal you want to work on."

7. Support questions—to provide emotional support.

   "How do you feel about _____?"

   "What could I (and/or your colleagues) do to help you with this issue?"

   "What are you doing for fun/exercise/stress relief?"

8. Observation questions (using data gathered—video, audio, notes, descriptions)—to help develop their ability to reflect on their work.

   "What is happening here?"

   "I heard/saw _____. Tell me about that."

9. Cause/effect questions—to help them see the relationships between their actions/students actions and the learning.

   "Why do you think _____ happened?"

   "What would happen if you did _____?"

10. Viewpoint questions—to expand the mentees' perspectives.

    "How might this look to a parent/administrator/the student?"

    "What do you think _____ was thinking at that time?"

    "When I saw _____, I wondered if _____ was a part of what was going on. Tell me your perspective of this." (Allows you to pose your "I think" comments.)

Role-Play: Using Guiding Questions for a Particular Purpose

Select a situation from Resource B in the back of this book and create a role-play, using some of the specific questions provided in Figure 3.7. Practice over time with your fellow mentors-to-be, using scenarios and modifying questions so that you feel comfortable not only using the guiding questions, but identifying when and where you should use them in a conversation with a mentee. The more you practice using guiding questions that move the mentee to higher levels of thinking and problem solving, the more effective the mentoring relationship will be.

Novice teachers need emotional support and they also need to be able to see the interactions in their classroom clearly. Meeting these two needs is a critical component of the mentor's role. If the mentor and novice teacher have developed a trusting relationship in which emotional support is provided and the mentor helps the mentee accurately view his or her work, the benefits for the students, the novice teacher, and the school are increased (Evertson & Smithey, 2000; Giebelhous & Bowman, 2000).

4

Addressing the Novice Teacher's Specific Needs

Depending on the knowledge and skills mentees bring to their 1st-year experience, they may have additional areas of concern. Besides providing emotional support, helping novice teachers view their classrooms realistically, and using guiding questions to extend thinking, there may be additional needs that a mentor must address. Everyone learns at his or her own pace, and some novice teachers need more support to help them move to the next level of proficiency. Generating an action plan and providing additional resources can address these specific needs. Whatever the level of knowledge and ability a new teacher has, all responses and comments must be presented to them honestly. Without honest feedback from their mentors, mentees will find it difficult to develop the skills necessary to respond to the challenges and issues they face in the classroom.

THE NEED FOR AN ACTION PLAN AND RESOURCES

At times, novice teachers may be unable to see how to improve their teaching, even after mentors have provided them with specific statements and observations from classroom interactions and have asked them guiding questions. They may recognize a problem or concern but be unsure how to solve it. It is important that beginning teachers realize that they are not expected to have all the answers but that they can access resources to help develop their effectiveness and find answers. They can then use these resources to develop an action plan.

A mentor can introduce resources using direct language (see Chapter 2) as a way to heighten mentees' awareness of an issue they haven't been able to recognize on their own. Reading about a management process or specific examples of cooperative learning and then discussing the resources with their mentor can help mentees become more acutely aware of issues they did not previously see as concerns. For example, mentors who wish their mentees to plan and structure cooperative learning more carefully might introduce them to *Joining Together* (Johnson & Johnson, 2002) and ask them to read a particular section of the book. Mentor and mentee can then discuss concepts from the text, and the mentor can request that concepts such as individual and group accountability be incorporated into the next cooperative learning lesson. Without an example, the mentee may not be able to conceptualize the mentor's requests or to understand the need to incorporate the ideas described by the mentor. A resource broadens the perspective of a topic or issue that might surface during observations and also provides examples beyond those the mentor can articulate. When mentors provide specific evidence via a resource, both they and their mentees have common ground upon which to base further conversation and development (Bleach, 1999; Chapel, 2003). In addition, the search for new resources and the discussion of new ideas can benefit mentors by stretching their thinking and enhancing their own learning (Gilles & Wilson, 2004).

Once novice teachers are able to recognize individual student needs, they need support to plan ways to address them. Many stall in their growth at this point because, although they recognize the needs, they are not sure what to do about them. Mentors must respond to the issues and concerns identified by mentees and specifically ask them how they plan to address the issue. This can be done after mentees have investigated the resources offered or in ongoing discussions while they are reading. Either way, it is vital that mentors help the novice teacher set up a plan for addressing concerns. To be effective in this role, mentors need to be aware of new ideas and methodologies so they can suggest appropriate and timely readings or workshops and connect mentees with teachers whose classrooms reflect the desired skill or method (Giebelhaus & Bowman, 2000).

If mentors do not know what to do about an issue, it is even more imperative that they find the appropriate resources and develop a plan with their mentees. Often mentors simply need to connect mentees with the individuals in a school system—the staff development director, the special education teacher, the school psychologist, fellow teachers—and help them to use these human resources to support their own work in the classroom. Novice teachers cannot be allowed to "wing it" or to ignore a problem. While mentors are not expected to know all the answers, it is important that they are able to locate the appropriate resources. By doing so, mentors convey to beginning teachers that learning how to address all the learners in the classroom is an ongoing process and demonstrate the process of lifelong learning (Moir & Bloom, 2003). If a mentee feels that his or her mentor does not know what to do, the novice certainly will not take action and may develop a pattern of learned helplessness. Mentors who participate in a search for answers are modeling the idea that finding answers to the needs posed by the students in a classroom is what good teachers do (Storms et al., 2000).

Once mentees convey to their mentors that they have seen an issue or problem but do not know what to do about it, or when mentors have determined that some additional support is needed to recognize and respond to an area of concern, an action plan needs to be created. An action plan can certainly be used at any time to identify specific goals, but it is especially important when mentees do not recognize how they need to modify or change their behavior. It is a document that identifies resources to be shared, steps to be taken, and a timeline for completion. Running a classroom requires a great deal of work, and novice teachers may not make it a priority to set aside time to work on issues or concerns. An action plan sets up an expectation and goals for achieving continued learning in a particular area.

The action plan may focus on accessing resources, may involve action research in the classroom, or may suggest a new strategy to try with particular students. It should be developed and agreed upon by both the mentor and mentee and can provide a focus for future observations and conferences. Figure 4.1 provides mentors with an example they can follow when creating their own action plans.

This is a simple plan; more complex issues need more detailed plans. An action plan provides mentees with a concrete process to address their concerns—and helps them learn to take action to address specific issues. Mentors can use the sample action plan as a guide. In creating a viable plan, both parties need to share their thoughts and listen to each other's ideas.

To deal with the situation outlined in the dialogue below, the mentor and mentee might come up with the following steps:

Step 1: Talk with the student's other teachers to determine whether the behavior is a pattern or if it is just occurring in this particular class.

Step 2: Talk with the counselor to see whether there are issues at home that might be impacting the student's behavior.

Step 3: Review homework assignments to determine whether there is a disconnect between the homework and the ability of the student.

Dialogue: Action Plan

DIALOGUE

A student never completes or attempts any homework. The student is bright and does well in class. The mentee is frustrated, and the student is failing because of this. The parents have been called, but while they are concerned, they don't know how or when the student does any of his homework. The new teacher wants to help the student succeed and learn but doesn't know what to do. What kind of action plan might you create in this situation? Sketch out a plan and share it with another mentor. Compare your ideas and consider what other possibilities might be included in the action plan. Use Figure 4.2 to develop your plan.

Figure 4.1   Example: Action Plan

After trying several ways to address the following issue, a mentee asks his mentor what to do about the situation. Together they develop this action plan. They agree on the timeline, and the novice teacher fills in the reflection/results/information section as he works through the action plan.

Issue or behavior	Strategies to address the situation	Resources	Timeline	Mentee reflections, results, or information
Mary, a third-grade student, is constantly shouting out answers, talking very loudly in class when not called on, and disturbing her classmates. Her fellow students do not want to include her in their play, so Mary forces her way into their games.	1. Check Mary's file or talk to her first- and second-grade teachers to determine if this pattern occurred in previous years.		Complete by next mentor meeting: _____ (date)	
	2. Read about similar behaviors.	*Emotional and Behavioral Problems: A Handbook for Understanding and Handling Students* (2005). Paul Zionts, Laura Zionts and Richard Simpson (Corwin Press)	Complete book in two weeks, by _____ (date)	
	3. Talk to the special-education teacher.	Set up visit with special-education teacher _____ (name), who can offer suggestions for how to help Mary.	Complete by next mentor meeting: _____ (date)	
	4. Discuss book and special-education teacher input with mentor and identify a strategy to use in the classroom.		Next mentor meeting scheduled for: _____ (date)	
Next steps based on completed task 1–4.	5. Implement behavior strategy based on the input from previous teachers, special-ed. teacher and/or ideas from text.	Use text as a reference during implementation of the new strategy.	Start behavior strategies by Monday, _____ (date)	
	6. Monitor the behavior plan for success and keep data on the number of times Mary disturbs class or play-mates over the next three weeks.		Gather data for the weeks of _____. (date) Review data after three weeks; have results ready to discuss by _____. (date)	

Signed: _____   _____   _____

(mentor)   (mentee)   (date)

Figure 4.2   Practice Action Plan

Issue or behavior	Strategies to address the situation	Resources	Timeline	Reflections
Student doesn't do homework and is failing because of it. Parents are concerned but have no suggestions.				
Next steps:				

Signed: _____   _____   _____

               (mentor)   (mentee)   (date)

This work would be completed in the first week after the initial conference, and the information gathered would serve as the basis for the teachers' next steps. If the mentee discovered that the student did complete her homework in other classes, or the counselor reported that the student complained that she was bored in this particular class, or all homework assignments had involved reinforcement and practice of skills that the student seemed to possess, then the following steps would be put into place:

Step 4: Mentee identifies enrichment or extension opportunities for the student to engage in as homework.

Step 5: Mentee sets up a contract with the student, which states that if the student can demonstrate her understanding of the concept being addressed by writing a brief statement or through a brief conference after class, the mentee can then move on to step 6.

Step 6: Mentee asks the student what she would like to do to extend her learning in this particular subject or area and assists the student in developing an independent study project for homework.

The mentor should keep in mind that the follow-up steps are directly related to the information gathered. If another set of answers had been discovered—for example, if this was a high school student, and the student was failing all classes, and the parents were concerned about the student's possible experimentation with drugs or alcohol—then the follow-up steps would be completely different. The goal of the novice action plan is to gather evidence and to respond to that evidence appropriately.

■ THE NEED FOR HONESTY

Beginning teachers need an honest appraisal of their work. To reiterate, it is not helpful for mentors to overwhelm novice teachers with several areas of concern at one time. However, it is equally as damaging for mentors to avoid describing problems. Mentors who understand the difficulties teachers face in the classroom and who have developed strong positive relationships with their mentees may feel uncomfortable pointing out negative aspects of their practice. However, if honest, exact descriptions are provided in a nonjudgmental way, mentees can learn from the experience and strengthen their skills. By failing to point out an area of concern, mentors allow mentees to continue practices that are ineffective or even harmful to students.

If mentors mirror classroom observations and ask guiding questions and the novice is still unaware of the area of concern, mentors need to be more directive and use specific, nonjudgmental language. Once mentees are aware of problems, action plans should be developed. If action plans are implemented but the problems continue, mentors should provide mentees with evidence that a change has not occurred and ask questions about what might be impeding their ability to work in this particular area. This should be done when mentors do not see mentees implementing action plans or when mentees' action plans do not produce the desired results. Mentors must speak honestly so that they clearly communicate their concerns and listen carefully so they hear what is behind the mentees' inability to solve the problem. Any lack of understanding or miscommunication at this point could undermine the effectiveness of the mentoring relationship.

If mentees cannot articulate why they are unable to effectively address a concern and complete the action plan, mentors need to consider other options (Young, Alvermann, Kaste, Henderson, & Many, 2004). If the issue is significant, mentors might consider bringing in another mentor to provide additional evidence and ideas. Mentors must honestly tell their mentees that it is helpful to get another perspective in order to view things more clearly. This will allow other individuals to intervene without making mentees feel like they are being ganged up on.

Mentors also might determine that an issue deserves ongoing attention. This would be the case if the issue pertains to a challenging student need that the mentee is not developmentally ready to address. Any skill that the novice teacher has not yet mastered should be considered for ongoing work. It must be agreed that the mentee will continue to focus on that issue, and the mentor may need to extend the time provided for that effort. By allowing time for continued effort and setting up long-range goals, mentors validate the time and effort needed for teachers to reach necessary levels of competence. Teachers do not perfect their skills in the first years of teaching. Effective educators always set goals for themselves to continue their learning, and mentors can help novice teachers develop this habit by identifying areas for ongoing work.

Mentors should review Figure 4.3 to see an example of long-range plans and goal setting.

Mentors can use the template in Figure 4.4 to develop long-range plans when mentees need additional time to accomplish their goal.

Figure 4.3   Example: Long-Range Plan

Emily has been trying to help Steve, her mentee, expand his use of assessment strategies. Although they have developed and worked through an action plan, Steve still is unsure about the use of alternative assessments. As the end of the school year approaches, Emily is concerned that Steve still does not feel comfortable using performance assessments.

She and Steve set up a long-range plan that will continue into his second year of teaching. Review their long-range plan and, with another mentor, discuss your reactions to developing such a plan or jot down your reflections on this issue.

Long-Range Plan

Mentee: _____*Steve Hanson*_____ Class: *Eighth-grade English*

Mentor: _____*Emily Shields*_____ Date: _____*04/21/05*_____

Author of plan: _*Emily Shields*_

1. *Identify the issue:*

   Steve is working on varying his forms of assessment. Paper-and-pencil unit tests on literature are his most comfortable format. Some students are not very successful with these assessments, yet they contribute well in class discussions of the literature. We talked about this a lot this year, and I suggested that additional or alternative methods of assessment should be investigated. Steve agreed.

2. *Briefly describe the action plan already in place:*

   Steve read and discussed articles recommended by the mentor on performance assessment (sections from resources listed below). He observed teachers using performance assessment and reviewed student work from those tasks. He was to devise a performance assessment for students to complete at the end of the next assigned novel, *Flowers for Algernon*.

3. *Describe the work the mentee has completed as a part of the action plan:*

   Steve completed the readings and discussed performance assessment with me. Students were asked to complete a book review after reading the novel, following class discussion. The book review was Steve's response to developing performance assessment. The resulting student work primarily reflected students' awareness of the plot of the book and the main characters. During a conversation with Steve, he stated that he felt that the information provided by the book review was similar to that produced in the the paper-and-pencil test, but that the circumstances (the students were allowed to complete the report at home) might have provided opportunities for outside assistance. Steve questioned the validity of the book review as an assessment. I said that the ability for students to articulate, in their own words, the key concepts from the book would be an example of performance assessment and suggested that he continue to try similar assessment formats. In addition, I suggested that next time the performance response or book review be written in class and that Steve should define expectations for the book review so students would be clear about the type of response he wanted from them.

4. *Record outside mentor's observations:* (Another mentor participated in conversations on the topic of assessment during new teacher meetings.)

   Conversations with Steve focused on his ideas about the purpose of assessment and the expectations for students regarding the books they read. It is clear that Steve is committed to ensuring that the students read and understand the novels and other readings in the curriculum. He identifies "student understanding" as the ability to identify key events and characters as well as the author's intent (theme). Teacher-directed class discussions and quizzes over each assigned chapter were also used by Steve to determine understanding. He seems unable to expand his repertoire of assessment strategies. Developing expectations for students beyond the knowledge and comprehension level would be an important next step for Steve.

5. *List long-term goals for continued learning in this area:* Both assigned mentor and outside mentor recommend that the mentee complete the following tasks:

   (a) Steve will continue to read about performance assessment and observe other teachers using this assessment format.

   (b) Within the next year, the district will be requiring that portfolios of student work be passed on to high school teachers, and collections of assessments will need to be included. With this in mind, Steve needs to develop at least one specific performance assessment, along with the purpose for the assessment and grading guidelines, for the final novel taught this year.

(Continued)

Figure 4.3 (Continued)

(c) Steve will sign up for the district's workshop on assessment that will be held this summer.

(d) Steve will set up times to plan with the other eighth-grade English teachers this summer and next fall in order to utilize their expertise. I will also set up times to help Steve with his planning.

6. *Estimate time frame estimated for goal completion:*

- Readings (see list below) will be completed by (date:_____), and we will plan to meet and discuss the books in early August (date: _____).
- Observations of _____ (teachers to be observed) will be completed by Steve before the end of the school year.
- Performance assessments for Steve's reading assignments for the rest of this year will be given to Emily when students receive them.
- Steve will attend the summer workshop on assessment.
- Emily will help get Steve connected so he can participate in planning with the rest of the eighth-grade teachers during the summer and throughout next school year.
- Emily will continue to observe and meet with Steve during the second year of teaching to follow up on these goals.

7. *Complete suggested readings:*

Performance Tasks, Checklists and Rubrics by Cindy Stergar. Published in 2005 by Corwin Press.
Classroom Assessment: Enhancing the Quality of Teacher Decision-Making by Lorin Anderson. Published in 2003 by Laurence Erlbaum Associations, Inc.
Great Performances: Creating Classroom Based Assessment Tasks by Larry Lewin and Betty Shoemaker. Published in 1998 by ASCD.

While many mentoring programs last only one year, some districts provide for continued connections during the second and third year of the novice teacher's employment, aiding the success of long-range goal planning. Even if mentees do not have a specific area of concern, setting up long-range goals can help their development by reinforcing the need for continual learning. Working and conversing with a peer who is also relatively new to teaching, or self-monitoring through the use of reflective journaling, also can be helpful in addressing long-range plans.

Although mentors must determine what to do when they feel their mentees are not meeting identified expectations, they also need to be realistic about those expectations. Few novice teachers are able to perfect all aspects of their practice in one year, so mentors may need to reconsider their view of what can be accomplished. If mentees are reflecting on their work, asking questions, and seeking ways to improve, they are providing a very significant indicator of their future success.

If mentors have serious concerns about their mentees' behavior or their dedication to their work, they must talk to them about these issues. Intervention may be needed if the mentor strongly believes that a mentee has inappropriate philosophical perspectives for a school context or has not exhibited any positive behavior change to meet identified long-term goals. For example, if a mentor has identified the need for a mentee to generate more specific lesson plans, but despite an action plan, conversations, and the creation of long-term goals, the mentee continues to come to class without any written plans, intervention would be warranted. Mentees whose behavior suggests that they are not serious about improving their teaching skills must be told that this behavior may keep them from becoming a successful teacher. Mentors often find this task extremely difficult, but they must remember that mentees have a responsibility to fulfill their role as learners.

Figure 4.4   Long-Range Plans

Complete this framework to identify ongoing goals.

1. Identify the issue:

2. Briefly describe the action plan already in place:

3. Identify work the mentee has completed as a part of the action plan:

4. Record outside mentor's observations (if applicable):

5. List long-term goals for continued learning in this area:

6. Estimate time frame for goal completion:

7. Complete the following readings:

Signed: _____   _____   _____
                (mentor)   (mentee)   (date)

At this point, a candid conversation with someone other than the mentor is needed. When this intervention is warranted, the supervisor usually gets involved in the process. For student teachers, this is the college supervisor, and for 1st-year teachers, it may be the director of the mentoring program, the staff development director, or perhaps another mentor. Mentors must remember that trust will be irrevocably destroyed if they convey concerns to the mentee's evaluator (Feiman-Nemser et al., 1999). It is always helpful, therefore, if mentors bring in a staff person or an administrator who is not directly evaluating the mentee. Another mentor or an administrator can be very frank with novice teachers and let them know that if they wish to continue to teach in that district/school they will need to work to develop their skills in the area of concern.

A principal from another building or a dean of students who is not involved in decisions about retaining staff at the mentee's school might also be brought in to provide an outside or unofficial evaluation. These individuals are the most appropriate choices for an outside evaluator. Their suggestions, which reflect what typical administrators are looking for during the evaluation process, might bear more weight than those of another mentor or a program director.

This type of intervention is based on the premise that the mentor's concern is valid and that the mentee has failed to address the concern or is unable to do so. If the mentor has an inaccurate view of the importance of some aspect of the novice teacher's work, the intervention or additional evaluation will point that out. Sometimes, mentors become fixated on a particular aspect of their mentees' development and fail to see the big picture. An intervention can verify whether an issue has indeed reached a level where concern is warranted. When mentoring breaks down and intervention is used, the effectiveness of the mentoring process will be severely crippled, and a new mentor with an unbiased perspective may need to be assigned.

The dialogue on page 63 outlines examples of cases that might lead to a need for intervention.

Very few mentoring situations reach an impasse where intervention is needed. There are processes a mentor can follow to create opportunities for a mentee's success, and every novice teacher has the ability to learn and grow. Mentors must believe in the power of supportive learning and work to help mentees move forward, even if the steps they take are small. This is an intensive process, and mentors need to be committed to providing this ongoing support for the novice teacher, despite the challenges and time commitment (Brooks, 2000). The goal is to help novices develop into effective educators; and if mentors use the processes discussed in this book, they can address all the individual needs that novice teachers bring to the classroom. These processes include the following:

- Providing evidence of classroom interactions (both positives and concerns)
- Using nonjudgmental language
- Providing opportunities for mentees to reflect on their work
- Providing guiding questions
- Being supportive and empathetic, yet honest
- Being direct when necessary
- Providing resources

Dialogue: Working Through an Impasse

DIALOGUE

Read the following situations and reflect for a few moments or role-play the scenarios with another mentor. Follow up by discussing (or writing) your thoughts on the questions that follow.

- A mentee believes that classrooms must be absolutely silent for learning to take place. Even when following an action plan that involves class projects and readings on active learning, the mentee constantly reprimands students for making noise.
- A mentee believes that learning can only take place through self-directed learning and does not provide any instruction for the students, even after reading and discussing various learning styles and noting the poor quality of student work.
- A mentee uses a disdainful tone and demeaning language with the students in the classroom. When tape-recorded, she seems unable to recognize how her language is affecting the students and implies it is the kids' fault they are not learning.

When considering your response to the situations listed above, keep in mind the processes that have been discussed in this chapter. These are cases where mentors have already tried options and are at the point where they need to be very directive. Think about the language you would use, and the examples and processes you might engage in to move the mentee beyond this impasse. There are no right answers, but as a mentor, you need to consider how you would use every interaction and tool available to you to communicate your concerns and offer direction.

Questions for Further Thinking

- Which issues are ones you would not compromise on as a mentor? What would be an example of an issue and the level of concern that you feel would require outside intervention?
- How would you proceed in your relationship with a mentee who held these beliefs?
- Who would you go to in your school or district for intervention? How would you facilitate intervention or evaluation?

- Setting up action plans to address areas for further growth
- Communicating concerns and issues honestly
- Setting up long-term goals for ongoing learning
- Using intervention if an impasse is reached

WHAT STUDENT TEACHERS NEED ■

The needs of student teachers are very similar to the needs of 1st-year teachers as identified in this chapter, and their mentors should try to meet all of the needs listed above. However, student teachers often feel added pressure because their mentors also serve as their evaluators. Sometimes they feel like someone is always looking over their shoulder. Mentors must allow student teachers to develop their own style, even if it is different from their own (Cowne & Little, 1999). This is challenging for the mentor, who will have to address the effects of the changes in teaching style, methods, or procedures that occur when the student teacher leaves the mentor's classroom. Some mentors/cooperating teachers are reluctant to fully support their mentees' development if it means disruption to the flow they have established in their classrooms.

However, to develop professional skills, mentees need to make curricular decisions and reflect on student responses. Mentors can take a more direct approach during the first days of student teaching, but mentees must have opportunities to make decisions on their own. Without the chance to develop their decision-making skills, to reflect on their choices, and to monitor and adjust, student teachers become dependent on others to tell them what to do. The first year of teaching is more successful when a student teacher has been allowed to take on all the duties of the classroom teacher with full support from his or her cooperating teacher.

Student teachers must be placed in the role of teacher, but this may be phased in at the beginning of their experience. Team teaching is an excellent way for mentors to provide student teachers with a gradual induction. In time, they are given more responsibility—adding classes and subject areas until they are handling all teaching duties. As the student-teaching semester draws to a close, they can slowly hand back classes to mentor-teachers who can then acclimate students to any inverse changes. A specific daily schedule for conferences is also vital to the support of student teachers. They need much more interaction with mentors than do 1st-year teachers, and if mentors do not keep up with daily discussions, the student teachers' performance can suffer.

Student teachers have another special and substantial need—finding their first job. The letter of recommendation from the cooperating teacher or mentor weighs heavily on their minds, causing them to be hesitant to ask questions or try things that might expose what they perceive as ignorance. Mentors who offer support and advice for job searching and interviewing can help ease their mentees' minds. By addressing these additional needs, mentors can successfully support the ongoing learning of their student teachers or mentees.

5

The Mentor's Lens

In order to provide novice teachers a view of their teaching and learning practices, mentors visit and observe protégé's classrooms. The mentor's goal for a classroom observation is to serve as a mirror, reflecting what occurs. Mentees get to see what is happening through their mentor's eyes. Depending on their teaching styles and interests, some mentors may focus on certain areas of mentees' practices more than others. Because of this natural focusing tendency, it is important that both know up front what *lens*—a description of professional practice—a mentor is using to view the classroom. Without a defined focal point, the mentor may overlook some of what is happening in the novice teacher's instructional practices by giving too much credence to a particular activity.

VIEWING TEACHING AND ■
LEARNING THROUGH A LENS

Many states have defined a set of standards for new teachers, and these standards act as a lens for viewing professional practice. Many mentors use their state or district standards as a lens when observing their novice teachers. Some mentoring programs develop their own standards. What is most important is that a lens is selected and used. Without a lens to provide a shared understanding of what constitutes effective teaching, a mentoring relationship may become unfocused and unproductive.

Several instruments are available for use as a lens, and most of these have similar components. Mentors need to be familiar with these components and consider how they describe a novice teacher's efforts. Rather than gathering evidence of classroom interactions randomly, mentors can use an instrument as a lens to focus their selection of evidence and help mentees identify areas for growth. Together, mentor and mentee can identify which components the mentor will focus on during an observation.

As time goes on, mentors may need to use guiding questions to help mentees see components they have not yet addressed in their teaching. If a mentee is resistant to a mentor's suggestions, a well-defined lens can give credence to the mentor's recommendations for growth. A lens also allows mentors to observe from a balanced perspective, even if their mentees' teaching style is unique or different from their own.

Mentors and mentees need to come to a common understanding about the lens used to observe a classroom. For example, if a district is using a particular model, it is imperative that mentors reflect the district's language and emphasis in their interactions with mentees by using that model, or lens, in their observations. If mentees are not developmentally ready for the detail and specificity implicit in a particular model, mentors can help them develop a higher level of awareness of the language and processes implicit in it by discussing the language and providing examples of teaching that exemplify the model. Mentors can do this by providing mentees with opportunities to observe teachers who effectively integrate the knowledge and skills indicated in the model and by following up with a discussion about the strategies used. The mentee can then try to replicate some of these processes. Mentors may initially choose to select a model, or lens, that is more appropriate for the mentee's level of learning and switch to the district's lens later in the year. No matter which approach is taken, mentees need to understand the organizational structure used to view their work. They must clearly understand what is expected of them, and this may require having some additional conversation and sharing resources (a description of the lens) prior to observation.

Although mentors have traditionally focused their attention on the classroom where the teacher's work is most apparent, planning is what creates effective teaching and learning. Positive, supportive interactions in the classroom do not happen randomly—teachers have to thoughtfully consider how to create a climate conducive to learning. The work teachers do has a huge impact on classroom effectiveness: Connecting with parents, working with colleagues, and continuing their own education are all characteristics of good teaching. Mentors need to look at their mentees' planning practices and professional interactions as well as what happens in the classroom.

Currently, nationally known instruments usually ask for evidence of a teacher's work in four broad areas: planning, instruction, classroom interactions, and professionalism. All of these lenses identify what novice teachers should know and be able to do, but none specifies an exact method. Some of the options available include the following models.

PATHWISE

The PATHWISE model was developed by Educational Testing Service (ETS) and came out of the work on the PRAXIS series of tests developed for states to use in licensing teachers. PATHWISE is a nonlicensing, evaluation, training and assessment program available from ETS (1995) that evolved from PRAXIS III, an assessment of classroom practices. The PATHWISE model consists of four domains that are outlined in Figures 5.1, 5.2, 5.3, and 5.4.

The formative observation forms for PATHWISE include criteria categorized as domains. Domains B and C are observed during class, while A and D are reviewed during conversations with the teacher. Mentors are to gather evidence of teacher behaviors that apply to each domain and subdomain.

Domain A (Figure 5.1) includes components of planning as they relate to students and content. This domain covers teacher interaction with students and how it affects their learning.

Domain B (Figure 5.2) is focused on creating a positive environment in the classroom.

Domain C (Figure 5.3) deals with teaching and enhancing learning by making students aware of goals, monitoring student learning, and making changes where necessary.

Domain D (Figure 5.4) concerns professionalism, with an emphasis on reflection and collaboration with colleagues and parents/guardians.

The training and assessment offered by PATHWISE is designed to create stable guidelines mentors can use to clearly and consistently see evidence of beginning teachers' work in the four domains. Training is offered via videotaped teaching episodes. Mentors observe and gather evidence, then compare their findings. Repeated practice and conversation help observers using PATHWISE develop a high degree of reliability in gathering

Figure 5.1   Domain A—Organizing Content Knowledge for Student Learning

A1—Becoming familiar with relevant aspects of students' background knowledge and experiences

A2—Articulating clear learning goals for the lesson that are appropriate for the students

A3—Demonstrating an understanding of the connections between the content that was learned previously, the current content, and the content that remains to be learned in the future

A4—Creating or selecting teaching methods, learning activities, and instructional materials or other resources that are appropriate for the students and that are aligned with the goals of the lesson

A5—Creating or selecting evaluation strategies that are appropriate for the students and that are aligned with the goals of the lesson

SOURCE: From PATHWISE™ Formative Observation Form. © 1995 by Educational Testing Service, Princeton, NJ. Reprinted with permission.

Figure 5.2   Domain B—Creating an Environment for Student Learning

B1—Creating a climate that promotes fairness

B2—Establishing and maintaining rapport with students

B3—Communicating challenging learning expectations to each student

B4—Establishing and maintaining consistent standards of classroom behavior

B5—Making the physical environment as safe and conducive to learning as possible

SOURCE: From PATHWISE™ Formative Observation Form. © 1995 by Educational Testing Service, Princeton, NJ. Reprinted with permission.

Figure 5.3   Domain C–Teaching for Student Learning

C1—Making learning goals and instructional procedures clear to students

C2—Making content comprehensible to students

C3—Encouraging students to extend their thinking

C4—Monitoring students' understanding of content through a variety of means, providing feedback to students to assist learning, and adjusting learning strategies as the situation demands

C5—Using instructional time effectively

SOURCE: From PATHWISE™ Formative Observation Form. © 1995 by Educational Testing Service, Princeton, NJ. Reprinted with permission.

Figure 5.4   Domain D–Teacher Professionalism

D1—Reflecting on the extent to which the learning goals were met

D2—Demonstrating a sense of efficacy

D3—Building professional relationships with colleagues to share teaching insights and to coordinate learning activities for students

D4—Communicating with parents or guardians about student learning

SOURCE: From PATHWISE™ Formative Observation Form. © 1995 by Educational Testing Service, Princeton, NJ. Reprinted with permission.

solid evidence. All of its domains are considered equally important for effective teaching, and the criteria within each domain are measurable against rubrics developed for PATHWISE. Mentors who use PATHWISE as a lens engage in a common set of experiences in their training that helps them view the classroom with a particular focus.

ETS defines PATHWISE as a formative tool and specifically states on the observation form that it is not to be used to make decisions about personnel. This caution is noteworthy, as mentors need to constantly guard against inquisitive supervisors who try to use mentors to gather information about beginning teachers. A formative assessment model, such as PATHWISE, is critical in mentoring (Feiman-Nemser et al., 1999). Using such a lens to provide a common language and a model helps measure ongoing learning and is very important in a mentoring relationship, but all data collected by the mentor must remain confidential. Mentees can choose to include the information in a portfolio or evaluation conference with a supervisor, but mentors may not disclose any information that could be used for evaluative purposes to supervisors or anyone else.

A Framework for Teaching

Charlotte Danielson worked on the PRAXIS project for ETS. Her book *Enhancing Professional Practice: A Framework for Teaching* (1996) describes a framework for teaching that also can be used as a lens to observe beginning teachers. Similar to PATHWISE, her framework identifies four key components of professional practice. Danielson encourages educators to reflect on their practice using the competencies identified in her framework. This model is intended for observation of all teachers, not just beginners; therefore, the components of professional practice in her model include more detail and specific descriptors than those in PATHWISE, enabling mentors to look even more closely at their mentees' work.

Her framework identifies the components that should be found in effective, professional teaching practice. Because they evolved from the early work on the PRAXIS tests, both it and PATHWISE have similar expectations. Descriptions of teacher behaviors that exemplify these expectations are available in Danielson's book. The descriptions are similar to the ETS PATHWISE training materials that discuss expectations. When a more detailed model, such as this one, is used with the novice teacher, initial conversations may need to be more general and focus on the main concepts. The specifics of the subcomponents can be addressed later through action plans and long-range goals.

Danielson's framework domains and related components are listed in Figures 5.5, 5.6, 5.7, and 5.8. Observers are to gather evidence that identifies the novice teacher's skill as it applies to each component and subcomponent.

Domain 1 (Figure 5.5) identifies components of professional practice, which include knowledge of content, of students, and of resources.

Domain 2 (Figure 5.6) provides criteria for creating a well-managed and organized classroom that supports student learning, creating a

Figure 5.5   Domain 1: Planning and Preparation

Component 1a: Demonstrating Knowledge of Content and Pedagogy
    Knowledge of content
    Knowledge of prerequisite relationships
    Knowledge of content-related pedagogy

Component 1b: Demonstrating Knowledge of Students
    Knowledge of characteristics of age group
    Knowledge of students' varied approaches to learning
    Knowledge of students' skills and knowledge
    Knowledge of students' interests and cultural heritage

Component 1c: Selecting Instructional Goals
    Value
    Clarity
    Suitability for diverse students
    Balance

Component 1d: Demonstrating Knowledge of Resources
    Resources for teachers
    Resources for students

Component 1e: Designing Coherent Instruction
    Learning activities
    Instructional materials and resources
    Instructional groups
    Lesson and unit structure

Component 1f: Assessing Student Learning
    Congruence with instructional goals
    Criteria and standards
    Use for planning

SOURCE: From *Enhancing Professional Practice: A Framework for Teaching.* © 1996 Used with permission of Charlotte Danielson and the Association for Supervision and Curriculum Development. The Association for Supervision and Curriculum Development is a worldwide community of educators advocating sound policies and sharing best practices to achieve the success of each learner. To learn more, visit ASCD at www.ascd.org.

Figure 5.6   Domain 2: The Classroom Environment

Component 2a: Creating an Environment of Respect and Rapport
　　Teacher interaction with students
　　Student interaction

Component 2b: Establishing a Culture for Learning
　　Importance of the content
　　Student pride in work
　　Expectations for learning and achievement

Component 2c: Managing Classroom Procedures
　　Management of instructional groups
　　Management of transitions
　　Management of materials and supplies
　　Performance of non-instructional duties
　　Supervision of volunteers and paraprofessionals

Component 2d: Managing Student Behavior
　　Expectations
　　Monitoring of student behavior
　　Response to student misbehavior

Component 2e: Organizing Physical Space
　　Safety and arrangement of furniture
　　Accessibility to learning and use of physical resources

SOURCE: From *Enhancing Professional Practice: A Framework for Teaching.* © 1996 Used with permission of Charlotte Danielson and the Association for Supervision and Curriculum Development. The Association for Supervision and Curriculum Development is a worldwide community of educators advocating sound policies and sharing best practices to achieve the success of each learner. To learn more, visit ASCD at www.ascd.org.

positive environment, and managing classroom procedures and student behavior.

Domain 3 (Figure 5.7) pertains to how teachers communicate, what techniques they use to engage students in the learning, and how they interact with and provide feedback to students.

Domain 4 (Figure 5.8) includes components that concern the professional duties related to teaching, such as professional development, monitoring student progress, and communicating with parents or guardians.

INTASC

The Council of Chief State School Officers has developed the Model Standards for Beginning Teacher Licensing and Development: A Resource for State Dialogue (1992). These standards, commonly referred to as the INTASC (Interstate New Teacher Assessment and Support Consortium) standards, are models for preservice teachers that identify what new teachers should know and be able to do following a successful student-teaching experience. The INTASC standards have been incorporated into standards-based teacher certification programs in numerous states in response to the No Child Left Behind Act, and they are aligned with the National Board for Professional Teaching Standards (NBPTS). INTASC defines 10 principles as standards for beginning teachers. These principles are designed to be a guide for all education programs. They also can serve as a lens for mentors to observe all novice educators, because perfecting these beginning standards is often an appropriate goal for 1st-year as well as

Figure 5.7   Domain 3: Instruction

Component 3a: Communicating Clearly and Accurately
   Directions and procedures
   Oral and written language

Component 3b: Using Questioning and Discussion Techniques
   Quality of questions
   Discussion techniques
   Student participation

Component 3c: Engaging Students in Learning
   Representation of content
   Activities and assignments
   Grouping of students
   Instructional materials and resources
   Structure and pacing

Component 3d: Providing Feedback to Students
   Quality: accurate, substantive, constructive, and specific timeliness

Component 3e: Demonstrating Flexibility and Responsiveness
   Lesson adjustment
   Response to students
   Persistence

SOURCE: From *Enhancing Professional Practice: A Framework for Teaching*. © 1996 Used with permission of Charlotte Danielson and the Association for Supervision and Curriculum Development. The Association for Supervision and Curriculum Development is a worldwide community of educators advocating sound policies and sharing best practices to achieve the success of each learner. To learn more, visit ASCD at www.ascd.org.

Figure 5.8   Domain 4: Professional Responsibilities

Component 4a: Reflecting on Teaching
   Accuracy
   Use in future Teaching

Component 4b: Maintaining Accurate Records
   Student completion of assignments
   Student progress in learning
   Non-instructional records

Component 4c: Communicating with Families
   Information about the instructional program
   Information about individual students
   Engagement of families in the instructional program

Component 4d: Contributing to the School and District
   Relationships with colleagues
   Service to the school
   Participation in school and district projects

Component 4e: Growing and Developing Professionally
   Enhancement of content knowledge and pedagogical skill
   Service to the profession

Component 4f: Showing Professionalism
   Service to students
   Advocacy
   Decision making

SOURCE: From *Enhancing Professional Practice: A Framework for Teaching*. © 1996 Used with permission of Charlotte Danielson and the Association for Supervision and Curriculum Development. The Association for Supervision and Curriculum Development is a worldwide community of educators advocating sound policies and sharing best practices to achieve the success of each learner. To learn more, visit ASCD at www.ascd.org.

student teachers. If mentors find the specificity of other models too over-whelming for their initial work with their mentees, the INTASC principles (Figure 5.9) might be especially helpful. During an observation, mentors are to gather evidence of a mentee's ability to meet each principle.

Using INTASC as a lens provides mentors with a starting point for creat-ing a big picture of beginning teachers' work. Another model can be used in addition to INTASC to look at the details more closely, or mentors and mentees can develop a means to explore one of the principles in-depth to provide a more specific focus. INTASC's principles parallel the domains of PATHWISE and the components of Danielson's framework, using different language to identify what a beginning teacher should know and be able to do.

Figure 5.9   INTASC Principles

Principle #1:

Teacher understands central concepts, tools of inquiry, and structure of the discipline(s) he or she teaches, and can create learning experiences that make these aspects of subject matter meaningful to students.

Principle #2:

The teacher understands how students learn and develop, and can provide learning opportunities that support their intellectual, social, and personal development.

Principle #3:

The teacher understands how students differ in their approaches to learning and creates instructional opportunities that are adapted to diverse learners.

Principle #4:

The teacher understands and uses a variety of instructional strategies to encourage students' development of critical thinking, problem solving, and performance skills.

Principle #5:

The teacher uses an understanding of individual and group motivation and behavior to create a learning environment that encourages positive social interaction, active engagement in learning, and self-motivation.

Principle #6:

The teacher uses knowledge of effective verbal, nonverbal, and media communication techniques to foster active inquiry, collaboration, and supportive interaction in the classroom.

Principle #7:

The teacher plans instruction based upon knowledge of subject matter, students, the community, and curriculum goals.

Principle #8:

The teacher understands and uses formal/informal assessment strategies to evaluate and ensure the continuous intellectual, social, and physical development of the learner.

Principle #9:

The teacher is a reflective practitioner who continually evaluates the effects of his or her choices and actions on others (students, parents, and other professionals in the learning community) and who actively seeks opportunities to grow professionally.

Principle #10:

The teacher fosters relationships with school colleagues, parents, and agencies in the larger community to support students' learning and well-being.

SOURCE: From *Model Standards for Beginning Teacher Licensing and Development: A Resource for State Dialogue* by The Interstate New Teacher Assessment and Support Consortium. Published in 1992 by the Council of Chief State Officers. Used with permission. The Interstate New Teacher Assessment and Support Consortium (INTASC) standards were developed by the Council of Chief State School Officers and member states. Copies may be downloaded from the Council's Web site at http://www .ccsso.org.

Dimensions of Learning

Some districts have embraced a broader, more detailed model for organizing teaching and learning. *Dimensions of Learning Teacher's Manual* (Marzano, Pickering, Arredondo, Blackburn, Brandt, & Moffett, 1992) provides one such model, and it, too, provides a detailed lens by which a mentor may look into a mentee's classroom.

The goal of *Dimensions of Learning* is to focus classroom interactions on higher-level learning, and it offers another way of looking at those interactions. Published by the Association for Supervision and Curriculum Development (ASCD), *Dimensions of Learning* provides a more detailed set of criteria to identify effective teaching behaviors. Books and training sessions offered by the ASCD are available to assist in teachers' understanding and use of the *Dimensions* model. However, *Dimensions* focuses on expanding student learning and does not address teacher professionalism and growth in other areas. This lens is often used more broadly within a school or district to consider what parts of the learning process need to be improved. The components of the *Dimensions* model cited by Brown (1995) appear here as Figures 5.10, 5.11, 5.12, 5.13, and 5.14.

Dimension 1 (Figure 5.10) deals with the components of creating a positive learning environment for students, including maintaining a comfortable and orderly classroom.

Figure 5.10   I. Dimension 1: Helping Students Develop Positive Attitudes and Perceptions About Learning

---

A. The instructor helps all students feel accepted.

B. The instructor helps all students develop a sense of comfort in the classroom.

C. The instructor has designed instruction so that it reinforces students' sense of order in the classroom.

D. The instructor helps students clearly understand assigned tasks.

E. The instructor helps students believe that they have the ability and resources to successfully complete assigned tasks.

SOURCE: From *Observing Dimensions of Learning in Classrooms and Schools* by John L. Brown, pp. 111–112, Figure 9.10. © 1995 Association for Supervision and Curriculum Development. Reprinted by permission. The Association for Supervision and Curriculum Development is a worldwide community of educators advocating sound policies and sharing best practices to achieve the success of each learner. To learn more, visit ASCD at www.ascd.org.

Dimension 2 (Figure 5.11) relates to the elements of teaching students how to retain and apply knowledge by providing students with support and reinforcement of their skills.

Figure 5.11   II. Dimension 2: Helping Students Acquire and Integrate Knowledge

---

A. The instructor has designed instruction to help students construct meaning for declarative knowledge (i.e., facts, concepts, generalizations, principles) through the use of a variety of interactive strategies.

B. Students receive support to organize and store declarative knowledge effectively.

C. The instructor introduces and reinforces essential procedural knowledge (i.e., skills, processes, procedures) through ongoing modeling, shaping, and internalizing that includes providing extensive practice opportunities.

SOURCE: From *Observing Dimensions of Learning in Classrooms and Schools* by John L. Brown, pp. 111–112, Figure 9.10. © 1995 Association for Supervision and Curriculum Development. Reprinted by permission. The Association for Supervision and Curriculum Development is a worldwide community of educators advocating sound policies and sharing best practices to achieve the success of each learner. To learn more, visit ASCD at www.ascd.org.

Dimension 3 (Figure 5.12) pertains to the components of helping students expand and deepen their knowledge through instruction that emphasizes higher-order thinking skills.

Figure 5.12   III. Dimension 3: Helping Students Extend and Refine Knowledge

A. Wherever appropriate, students receive instructional support to "own" essential knowledge through activities requiring thoughtful application.

B. The instructor's questions focus on higher-level thinking and processes, rather than exclusive emphasis on knowledge/recall.

C. Students receive support to understand and apply important thinking processes such as the following:

- Comparison
- Classification
- Induction
- Deduction
- Analyzing errors
- Constructing support
- Abstracting/pattern recognition
- Analysis of perspectives

SOURCE: From *Observing Dimensions of Learning in Classrooms and Schools* by John L. Brown, pp. 111–112, Figure 9.10. © 1995 Association for Supervision and Curriculum Development. Reprinted by permission. The Association for Supervision and Curriculum Development is a worldwide community of educators advocating sound policies and sharing best practices to achieve the success of each learner. To learn more, visit ASCD at www.ascd.org.

Dimension 4 (Figure 5.13) refers to how teachers engage their students in learning related to real-life skills.

Figure 5.13   IV. Dimension 4: Meaningful Use of Knowledge

A. Where appropriate, the instructor involves students in long-term, self-directed, experience-based learning activities that reflect real-world roles and situations.

B. Where appropriate, the instructor engages students in meaningful-use tasks designed to reinforce their ability to use the following thinking operations:

- Decision making
- Investigation
- Problem solving
- Experimental inquiry
- Invention

SOURCE: From *Observing Dimensions of Learning in Classrooms and Schools* by John L. Brown, pp. 111–112, Figure 9.10. © 1995 Association for Supervision and Curriculum Development. Reprinted by permission. The Association for Supervision and Curriculum Development is a worldwide community of educators advocating sound policies and sharing best practices to achieve the success of each learner. To learn more, visit ASCD at www.ascd.org.

Dimension 5 (Figure 5.14) is concerned with the ways that teachers can encourage learning and intellectual growth in students.

All of these models identify key components of good teaching. When observed in the classroom, these various principles, domains, components, or dimensions all indicate effective practices. Mentors must keep in mind that although it is easy to use these criteria solely to determine what novice teachers cannot do, they should be used as a formative evaluation

Figure 5.14   V. Dimension 5: Developing and Using Productive Habits of Mind

A. The instructor models effective thinking skills and behaviors.

B. The instructor encourages students to reflect on their own thinking and monitor their own comprehension.

C. The instructor has designed classroom activities to reinforce students' ability to be self-regulated in their thinking, including planning, use of resources, sensitivity to feedback, and evaluating the effectiveness of their own actions.

D. The instructor encourages students to be effective critical thinkers, including seeking accuracy and clarity, being open-minded, and restraining impulsivity.

E. The instructor encourages students to be creative, to express their own opinions, to push the limits of their knowledge, and to generate new ways of viewing a situation.

SOURCE: From *Observing Dimensions of Learning in Classrooms and Schools* by John L. Brown, pp. 111–112, Figure 9.10. © 1995 Association for Supervision and Curriculum Development. Reprinted by permission. The Association for Supervision and Curriculum Development is a worldwide community of educators advocating sound policies and sharing best practices to achieve the success of each learner. To learn more, visit ASCD at www.ascd.org.

to determine areas for beginning teachers to direct their learning. Without a lens to focus a classroom observation, mentors and mentees can overlook areas of strength or miss areas where further learning is needed.

In some cases, mentors may be able to select the lens, or model, that will be used during observations by comparing the models to determine the best fit. The following analysis (Figure 5.15) can help them decide what model will be the most comfortable, and completing the comparison chart can help visualize more clearly the components of each potential lens.

If a district already has selected one of these models as its lens, mentors may still want to compare the models in this text to broaden their own understanding of these well-known descriptions of professional practice. It also might be helpful for mentors to incorporate other ideas from the various models to expand conversations with mentees about teaching and learning. Mentors can make their classroom observations highly useful and helpful to their mentees by developing an understanding of how to use lenses. Practicing applying lenses, using guiding questions, and reflecting what is observed in the classroom helps mentors prepare for this work with their mentees.

Figure 5.15   Analysis of the Lenses

Review the models presented and jot down your answers to the following questions.

Compare the models. How are they similar? How are they different?

Which model do you find most compatible with your teaching? Why?

Which one would you feel most comfortable using in a mentoring situation? Why?

Depending on the developmental level of your mentee, which model would you utilize? Why?

Share your perspective with another mentor, then list your observations below to create a comparison chart.

PATHWISE   Framework

_____   _____

_____   _____

_____   _____

_____   _____

_____   _____

INTASC   Dimensions

_____   _____

_____   _____

_____   _____

_____   _____

_____   _____

6

The Conferencing Cycle

After mentors and mentees have developed a comfortable level of trust and identified a lens to use for observation, they are ready to start the conferencing cycle. While all discussions of classroom practice are helpful, the need for novice teachers to see clearly what is happening in their own classroom requires mentor observations. The pre-observation, observation, and post-observation cycle provides a process for gathering such data.

THE PRE-OBSERVATION CONFERENCE ■

In the first phase of the conferencing cycle, the pre-observation conference, mentees inform their mentors of what will be happening in their classroom, and then both parties identify what the focus of that particular observation will be. This conference should take place close enough to the observation so that mentees have their plans for a particular lesson completed. During the conference, mentees should identify the objectives for the lesson, articulate their reasons for choosing these goals, and describe the steps they will follow or the structure they will use to engage the students in the learning. They should also identify how they plan to determine whether the students are successful in meeting objectives. Both parties should be aware of the lens that is being used. For example, if Danielson's framework for teaching (Danielson & McGreal, 2000) will be used, mentees will know that Component 1a requires them to demonstrate their knowledge of content and pedagogy. The preconference provides a time for novice teachers to articulate what they know about content and pedagogy as they describe their plans for the upcoming lesson.

In the initial observation, mentors should identify one or two components from the lens they are using as a focus, so the novice teacher is not overwhelmed. In later observations, mentors can gather evidence for all components of the selected model. The choice of a lens provides a clear focus for the pre-observation conversation: mentees are made aware of the specifics they need to identify in planning their classroom practice, and mentors know that they will need to ask guiding questions related to that area if the mentees do not address the components themselves.

The pre-observation conference is also a time for mentors to clarify anything they hear from their mentees that they are unsure about and to probe with guiding questions when they do not hear enough about a particular aspect of the lesson. This conversation should provide the mentor with some understanding of the mentee's planning skills. The give and take of this interaction allows mentees to expand their thinking about the choices they have made for this lesson. By clarifying the rationale for their plans and carefully addressing the details, novice teachers can be more successful when teaching the lesson.

A classroom observation should never take place without a pre-observation conference. The conference might lead to the creation of a refined lesson plan, or it might indicate to the mentor that the mentee needs some additional ideas. Observing a lesson without prior conversation can lead to misconceptions about the mentee's plans. For example, a mentor who might focus solely on management issues for a lesson in which the mentee was working to use active learning might fail to completely understand what occurred in the classroom, because his or her focus was only on management. Mentees can also mention if there is something specific they want the mentor to focus on during the observation.

A pre-observation conference does not always need to be a face-to-face interaction, although talking directly will enhance the communication and enable both parties to clearly "hear" the nonverbal aspect of the conversation. The pre-observation conference can also be in writing—by sharing lesson plans and offering written details to explain the rationale for the method and content selection. An e-mail exchange of plans and feedback can provide a convenient way for novice teachers and mentors to review what is going to happen in an observation. Electronic mentoring alone cannot provide all the support novice teachers need, but using e-mail can help both individuals in the mentoring relationship manage their time more effectively (Butler & Chao, 2001; Sinclair, 2003). If scheduling conflicts prevent a meeting prior to the lesson, a phone conversation is another option. At the very least, a brief conversation based on written comments and plans can help prevent misunderstandings and ensure that both individuals are on the same page at the start of the lesson.

The following dialogue demonstrates examples of questions that can be asked in a pre-observation conference to gather information about the upcoming observation and the type of focus these questions represent. The focus for each observation may vary according to the lens used.

If mentees cannot provide answers to some of these questions during the pre-observation conference, they may not be sufficiently prepared for the lesson. In this case, further discussion may be needed, and mentors

Dialogue: Preconference Questions

DIALOGUE

Review the sample questions listed below and discuss them with another mentor, or reflect on how they might impact a pre-observation conference.

(Note the attempt to avoid language that could be misinterpreted by the mentee.) The type of information the question is attempting to discover follows each question in parentheses. Mentors can use such questions to gather evidence about their mentees' planning skills.

What is it you want your students to know and/or be able to do at the end of this lesson? (objective/knowledge of content)

Why did you choose this particular focus for your lesson? (purpose)

How do you think your students will do with this lesson? (knowledge of students)

How have you created connections between this lesson, yesterday's lesson, and tomorrow's lesson? (prior knowledge)

How are you planning to carry out_____ [specify the instructional strategy]? (knowledge of instructional practices)

How will you know that the students have met your goals? (assessment)

What would you like me to look for in this lesson? (self-knowledge; reflection)

may need to directly ask that some additional components be added to the lesson. Some authors of lenses used for the conferencing cycle provide materials and forms for novice teachers to complete prior to the preconference. It is important to have the preconference discussion and to identify a lens, but too much required paperwork for beginning teachers and mentors can be burdensome in this time-intensive process (Brooks, 2000). Keeping the preconference brief, concise, and focused is important.

The purpose of the pre-observation conference is to broaden the mentor's awareness of the lesson that will be observed, but this discussion may not fully reveal the depth of the mentee's planning. Mentors should try to help mentees articulate the rationale for their plans and offer guidance, but often the full details of planning are not uncovered until after the lesson is taught. This is why the full conference cycle—pre-observation, observation, and post-observation—should be completed before mentors draw any conclusions.

THE OBSERVATION ■

When mentors are observing a class, their goal is to be unobtrusive so that what occurs in the classroom is no different from what would occur if they were not present. They need to position themselves in the classroom so they can see both the teacher and the students. It is also helpful if the mentor can avoid being constantly in the students' sight. Usually this means taking a seat in the back of the room, although sitting to the side is also an option. Mentors can move if students are placed in groups or if the activity in the room changes location in order to see and hear comments made by the teacher and students. Some mentors prefer to remain anonymous during the observation, but students are naturally curious about having another teacher present. It is helpful if mentors offer an introduction or brief explanation to help students view observations as a normal part of the teaching and learning process.

During the observation, mentors need to gather evidence of what is happening. Figure 3.3 in Chapter 3 is an example of an informal observation form, and several other tools that can be used to gather data during the observation are described in Chapter 7. While note-taking is important, mentors should not be so intent on transcribing that they fail to watch and listen carefully. Whatever means they use to gather evidence, their goal is to remain objective and gather information to help mentees examine and reflect on their practice. The observational focus can be based on a request made by a mentee who wants to gather information about a particular aspect of his or her teaching, or it can be determined by the mentor's use of the identified lens.

■ THE POST-OBSERVATION CONFERENCE

After the observation, mentors and mentees get together to talk about the evidence gathered. This data should be shared without interpretation. The goal of the post-observation conference is to help mentees reflect on what happened in the lesson, to think about why something did or did not occur, and to consider other options or ideas for the future. Mentors serve as a mirror and reflect what happened in the classroom for the novice teacher through the data they gather. The mentor may need to use guiding questions to assist and direct the novice teacher's analysis of the lesson. These questions also can be used as a follow-up to help expand the conversation beyond a mentee's original thoughts and comments.

Based on the data gathered and the mentee's reflection on that evidence, mentors ask their mentees what they plan to do next. These steps can be incorporated into an action plan to help mentees continue to enhance their skills or may be informally noted for future reference. The next observational cycle should then be based upon issues identified during the postconference. During each subsequent observation, mentees should attempt to apply to the new lesson what they learned from the previous observation.

In order for pre- and post-observation conferences to be effective, mentors and mentees must have developed a trusting relationship, and mentors must use effective communication skills. No matter how much data are gathered and how many wonderful ideas mentors may offer to novice teachers, mentees will not be able to listen and respond to these issues if they do not have a trusting relationship with their mentor or are fearful of being evaluated on evidence from the observation. The observational cycle is intended to be formative and should be used as the basis of ongoing growth and development. No matter what lens mentors use during the observational cycle, honest, open, and trusting communication enables beginning teachers to think carefully about their teaching and make a conscious effort to develop their skills in certain areas.

The following practice dialogues can be role-played by mentors either with or without a lens to help focus the conversation. If mentors are not able to do so with a colleague, they should write out what they might say to the mentee portrayed in the scenario as if they were speaking directly to that person. These dialogues are meant to help mentors become familiar and comfortable with the feedback they give during the conferencing process.

There is more than one way to respond to the pre- and post-observation scenarios in Figures 6.1 and 6.2. Using these scenarios gives mentors practice considering *what* they are going to say and *how* they will say it when responding to a mentee. In addition, mentors get practice reading between the lines to interpret what a mentee says, another important mentoring skill (Orland, 2000). When mentors are in a real conference setting, they have to make immediate decisions. This dialogue helps them think about all of their options for responding to various situations and to practice doing so. Mentors should use this opportunity to carefully consider their responses to what they hear and see in these pre- and post-observation scenarios. This will enhance their ability to provide nonjudgmental support in a way that encourages and invites the novice teacher to respond.

There are no "right" answers for the scenarios outlined in Figures 6.1 and 6.2, but mentors will sharpen their own thinking skills as they rehearse their responses. Practicing their verbal responses provides mentors with a chance to hear and consider their comments and to weigh the endless reasons for mentees' behavior as well as options for their own replies. In addition, taping these role-plays and listening to them can provide helpful feedback to mentors as they hone their skills.

Dialogue: The Observation Cycle

DIALOGUE

Select a lens from Chapter 5 or one your school has developed for use in your mentoring program. Apply the lens in the following pre- and postconference scenarios. Once you select a lens, be prepared to use it as a guide for your conference questions. If you do not use a lens, consider what you will use as a basis for your conversation about the novice teacher's upcoming lesson.

Read through the descriptions in Figures 6.1 and 6.2. What do you see and hear in these situations? What guiding questions would you ask in these conferences to encourage reflective thinking by your mentee?

After you have reviewed the scenarios, take turns role-playing the parts of the mentor and mentee with a colleague. As the mentee, try to role-play as if you have limited understanding of your work, so the mentor is challenged to ask appropriate questions. When you are the mentor in the role-play, generate questions and use appropriate communication skills. If you are writing your response, consider all the possible reasons for the mentee's behavior and describe your response.

Figure 6.1   Pre-Observation Situations

1. During the pre-observation conference, your mentee seems distracted and shifts nervously in his chair. As you ask about his objectives and plans for the lesson, he mentions that he and his girlfriend have decided to get married during the winter break. You ask about the wedding plans, and then shift the conversation back to the lesson. The mentee presents several pages of typed lesson plans and says that he hopes you will look at how he is using questioning in his class, as he thinks he might be focusing on only a few people. "Some of these fifth graders can really provide some interesting answers, and I think I am relying on a few of the smarter ones to carry the discussion," he states. After you talk about what he has planned to help involve all the students in the discussion, he says that he hopes he has time to do all of this planning, considering the approaching wedding and everything. He adds that he never realized how long it would take to plan for each day's learning.

2. For several days you have tried to set up a time to talk with your mentee prior to today's observation. She has been busy and backed out of these scheduled meetings, so you are now talking with her during the passing period right before you are scheduled to observe the lesson. She tells you that she has everything organized, but that she will not really be teaching today as students are presenting information from their reports on explorers. She says there really is no need for a lesson plan or conversation about the lesson prior to the observation because of this student-centered activity.

3. Your mentee has been exceptional with whole-class instruction. You would like him to try to incorporate some cooperative learning into his teaching. You have shared and discussed several articles on the subject, and after your last observation, the mentee said that he would plan to use some cooperative learning strategies in future lessons. As you talk with him about the lesson you will be observing, you note that it is, again, a whole-class lesson.

4. As you discuss the upcoming observation with your mentee, she refers several times to one particular student, Taylor, who really "bugs her." The lesson plan, part of a unit on healthy eating, is well planned. Students have been recording their food intake for several days and today will compare their food journal to descriptions of healthful diets using a Venn diagram. As you conclude your conversation, the teacher says that she expects that Taylor will not have anything done.

5. You have been working with your mentee for several weeks, and this is your first visit to his second-grade class. As you discuss the upcoming observation, the teacher says, "I really want to be clearer with my directions. I think that I often say things in a somewhat confusing way, so my struggling students don't know what to do!" You tell him that you will look closely at this and see if you can gather some information on that for him. You note that he has tested and divided his students by reading ability. You ask him how he came to this decision. He replies that he really likes reading groups because it is easier to address the common needs of students rather than worry about all of them at once.

6. The physical education teacher has planned a culminating tournament following a unit on badminton. When you ask about how he is organizing the games, he says, "I really wasn't sure how to put the teams together. I want all the kids to be challenged to play well, but there are some kids that really are awful and some who excel in the game. At first I thought about mixing up the ability levels in each team, but I didn't want some of the more athletic kids to get mad at teammates who missed returns or serves. So I figured that it might be good to put kids of equal ability together so they wouldn't get frustrated with one another. I could tell you right now which teams will be in the final match, but at least everyone is going to be playing on a team where they will be able to participate equally. I'm just not sure this is the best way to do it."

7. Working with the primary grades as the special education teacher, your mentee has planned a pull-out session for a group of four second-grade boys who are falling further and further behind in reading. She wants to give them some specific prereading and during-reading strategies. "It is hard to do this within the whole class. I think I can get the boys to really focus and practice these strategies if we work alone." When you ask her about how the boys are doing in the class otherwise, she says, "They don't do their homework, even the modified work I give them. So it's hard to know how they are doing."

As mentors plan their response to these situations, they should think about the words and the tone of voice needed to convey their feelings in a supportive way. In addition, mentors should review the communication processes they want to use when asking questions to probe further into what would be happening in the lesson (preconference) or when discovering why things occurred the way they did (postconference).

Figure 6.2   Post-Observation Situations

1. A new teacher in a seventh-grade English class uses a questioning tone in all of her conversations with students. She asks them if they would like to be quiet or if they would like to start their work, and they respond by ignoring her. It takes most of the lesson just to get the students organized and working. Her lesson was to be a discussion of a novel, and the stated objective was for the students to "understand how the book's theme relates to their lives." She put the students in groups and gave them each a chapter to talk about. No discussion guidelines were provided. She then asked students to generate ideas about the book's impact on their lives and to have their ideas ready for tomorrow. She gave students the rest of the class to complete the work.

2. A teacher in a fourth-grade classroom wanted his students to write descriptive sentences. He gave each table-group a set of cards that had an adjective, a verb, or a noun printed on it and asked each group to put together the most descriptive sentence it could, using the words given. The groups taped their sentences together and put them up on the wall for the rest of the class to see. The students selected the sentences that they felt were the most descriptive. Students were then asked to write descriptive sentences on their own.

3. A high school science teacher assigned her students a reading from the text that described plant and animal cells and included directions for a cell exploration lab. She gave her students leaf samples and told them to follow the directions in the text, and then write up a lab report on their findings. Students followed the directions and created slides of leaves to depict plant cells. They also created a slide of animal cells using scrapings taken from inside their mouths. When this was done, students were then told to examine these slides under a microscope and identify the differences between the two cell types, using the text and their lab results to support their answers. Students were given a template for the lab report that asked them to draw the cells as they saw them through the microscope.

4. A sixth-grade math teacher asked his students to create a survey to gather data to be displayed in a graph. The students decided to ask their classmates about their favorite school lunch items and created several questions to ask them at lunch. During this lesson, students graphed their results. Their work included some graphs that had tally marks for all responses, some with averages, some with comparisons. There were pie charts, bar graphs, and line graphs. Before the students began working on their graphs for today's class, the teacher told them they needed to use the most appropriate method to clearly display their results. After the teacher collected the graphs, he told the students that they were going to be graded on neatness.

5. The ninth-grade English class you just observed was the loudest you have ever heard. The teacher was leading a whole-class discussion on *Romeo and Juliet*. Conversations were going on throughout the lesson, several students were doing other work, and those that were paying attention kept saying "This is dumb," "How do you know that is what he said?" and "Why do we have to read this junk anyway?" The teacher kept going, ignored all remarks, and summarized each scene in the play for her students.

6. The special education teacher, your mentee, was working in a fourth-grade classroom during a social studies class. Students were reading a trade book about railroads and trains, and the teacher was asking them to share any stories or experiences they had regarding trains. The special education teacher was helping her student read sections of the text and underline and define the words he didn't know. The student did not participate in the generation of ideas about trains, although you heard him excitedly tell the teacher several things about trains. The teacher had replied, "We need to focus on the reading, James."

7. The tenth-grade choir was rehearsing a new song. While the teacher worked with the sopranos, the rest of the class talked loudly, sometimes tossing things at each other across the room. The teacher repeatedly turned and told the class to be quiet, saying that they needed to be respectful while one of the sections was working and that they should be looking over their music. A few seconds after each reprimand, the class was back chatting as loudly as before. This went on all lesson long as the teacher worked with each group on a difficult section of the music.

Several responses to each scenario are possible. For example, the conversation and dialogue following the second pre-observation situation could include these thoughts: Mentors are irritated that the mentee does not seem to be able to find the time to connect with them; they have the feeling that she does not want to talk to them at all. Nevertheless, they still need to convey warmth and understanding as they talk to the mentee and to let her know that they will discuss things further after the lesson. The mentee in this scenario may be afraid of the mentoring process or fearful that she will not do well, so she is avoiding the situation. Acknowledging potential emotions is as important as providing examples of how to link the assessment (of the student presentation) with an objective (perhaps student public speaking as well as research and developing a knowledge base). However, there are many ways to say this, and many ideas that could be shared.

In addition, in this pre-observation situation, although mentors may be concerned when the mentee states that there is no need for a lesson plan for this activity, it is important that they not show frustration through what they say or their tone of voice. The mentor can, however, be a bit more directive during the postconference and point out the need for planning and that it is helpful to set up a schedule for observational visits. It would also be important to explain that the mentor will be coming in to talk at least once a week (or whenever the mentor's schedule permits regular meetings). Mentors could also empathize with the fact that it is disconcerting to have someone watching during a lesson while communicating to the mentee that they want to make their classroom visits a supportive learning experience.

During the post-observation conference that would inevitably occur following the lesson described in the second pre-observation situation, the mentor would want to point out that, whether or not the mentee has been able to articulate them, there are reasons for the decisions she makes in the classroom. The mentor could then ask why the teacher asked the students to give reports, if there was preteaching before the students were assigned the reports, whether the reports were going to be assessed, and if so, how. These types of guiding questions point out to the mentee that any student presentation is a part of a larger objective and that she needs to be able to identify the reasons for making decisions about what goes on in the classroom.

If the mentee in this role-play is not able to give any answers or provide any reasons for the decisions that led up to this class, the mentor needs to provide some examples. The mentor might say, "The students were investigating _____. This is a part of the curriculum, and so you seem to be checking their understanding of the topic by having them research and provide information to their classmates. This is a form of assessment, and as all assessment is linked to an objective, I am wondering what your objective was for this lesson." Again, a supportive but firm tone is necessary so that the mentee hears clearly that he or she needs to have objectives and reasons for what occurs in the classroom and that those are best captured in some form of a lesson plan.

Mentors might want to provide, as resources, several different formats of lesson plans that they have used or are familiar with so the mentees have some options. Some mentees are leery of using a complex lesson plan format because making one is so time-consuming. Mentors may need to offer some ideas for abbreviated lesson plans to help with time management if novice teachers are feeling overwhelmed. The goal is to help them create effective lesson plans that will guide them as they teach.

Mentors will be more effective if they develop the ability to use the conferencing cycle to provide feedback to the novice teacher. By practicing applying lenses and using guiding questions within the context of the conferencing cycle, they will enhance the learning of novice teachers and enable them to develop the skills to observe, reflect, and problem-solve on their own.

7

Data-Gathering Techniques and Tools

Imagine that a mentor walks into a classroom and takes a random snapshot that includes all of the students and the teacher. What might this snapshot tell the mentor about the teaching and learning going on in that room? The photo might show two students facing each other, engaged in conversation, while the rest of the students are facing the teacher and holding their pencils to their notebooks. Would it be correct for the mentor to assume that the two students who are talking are off task and chatting about something other than the lesson? Should the mentor assume that all the students looking at the teacher are engaged in the lesson? The mentor cannot be sure, not knowing what is being said. A mentor has to hear the conversation to reflect on the teaching and has to talk to those involved to know what they are thinking. Gathering data about what goes on in a classroom means going beyond taking a quick snapshot.

As described in Chapter 6, the observation cycle includes a conversation before and after the mentor's visit to the classroom. The focus of the observation should be identified during the pre-observation conference, and these issues should be the main focus of the post-observation conference as well. In other words, the mentor and the mentee talk about what will occur in the lesson, then the lesson is taught, and then they discuss whether what was expected to happen actually did. As they confer about the lesson, mentors use the predetermined lens to focus their conversation. It is important that they facilitate reflection by describing specific things that happened in the classroom. Data-gathering techniques and tools can be used to help focus the discussion by providing evidence that describes what the mentor saw and heard (Glickman, Gordon, & Ross-Gordon, 1997).

A mentor needs to gather specific evidence to be a mirror that reflects the classroom interactions to the novice teacher. Then mentors need to clearly communicate what they observed so mentees can think about why things happened a particular way. Without evidence, this conversation can become centered on what mentors thought they observed rather than what actually occurred and they can form opinions and judgments that might not be accurate. Having specific data and evidence from a lesson is helpful when formulating guiding questions or developing an action plan. Data provide a more accurate mirror to help novice teachers view their practice more clearly. They will need to look at the data—the evidence gathered during the observation—and reflect on what occurred. Considering the significance of the data gathered in a classroom observation can help mentees develop their own problem-solving skills and assist mentors as they offer suggestions and guidance (Moir & Bloom, 2003).

■ QUALITATIVE VERSUS QUANTITATIVE DATA

Mentors need to be unbiased recorders of events in a classroom. Qualitative data-gathering focuses on describing classroom interactions from a 360-degree perspective. Quantitative observation involves counting, diagramming, and more structured forms of gathering evidence. Both processes can be helpful in gathering information for novice teachers to consider as they think about their practice (Glickman, Gordon, & Ross-Gordon, 1997). However, qualitative observations, which focus more on open questions than focused expectations, are a good way to begin when a mentor is first observing a mentee. Later, if more specific information is requested by the novice teacher or suggested by the mentor, quantitative data can be gathered.

■ SCRIPTING

Scripting involves taking notes about what happens during a lesson. Mentors sit in a location in the classroom that provides them with a good view of the students and the teacher and write down what they see and hear. Any interpreting of classroom interactions done by mentors during scripting should be noted as such, so mentees have the opportunity to respond and clarify.

A scripted statement, such as "The teacher intimidated the students with her reprimands," is an interpretive statement. The mentor has no idea if the students were really intimidated and is interpreting what was seen or heard. What mentors should provide, through noninterpretive scripting, is simply a description of what they saw and heard. This same situation might be scripted in this way: "The teacher said, 'Get your homework out right now! No more fooling around or I will have to keep some of you in from recess today!' Students looked startled; all immediately took out their work."

During the post-observation conference, the mentor might show the mentee the notes or read them aloud and ask, "I wondered if the students might have been a little surprised by your comments." At this point, the mentee can respond and clarify or explain the context. For example, perhaps this was a procedure that the class had been focusing on for several days, and the teacher felt the students should have been able to get to work. Or the mentee might respond that she did not realize she used those words and tone. In either case, the mentor can then ask guiding questions to facilitate the mentee's reflective thinking, such as the following:

- "How did you intend to identify those students who would be held in for recess if they hadn't gotten out their assignments?"
- "If you followed through on this consequence, who would stay with the students who were kept in for recess?"
- "Would you keep all of the students in for recess?"
- "Is there another way you could help students be accountable for following through on your requests?" (A mentor whose mentee needs more support can offer a more directive response, such as suggesting having a time schedule or a daily agenda on the board so that students know when it is time to get out their homework. Or the mentor could suggest that the mentee write the directions on the board and direct students to follow them.)

Mentors can facilitate a mentee's reflective thinking by providing evidence or data from the mentee's classroom and asking him or her to respond to it. Mentors can ask follow-up questions, such as "What about this?" "What do you think this means?" and "Why do you think this happened?" after presenting the mentee with evidence of classroom interactions. Again, mentors need to avoid the urge to editorialize about why they think certain classroom interactions occurred.

The evidence gathered should reflect both the areas of concern and the strengths of the teaching interaction. This is the benefit of using the scripting technique—because the goal is to write down all interactions, all events are noted. With this complete overview, mentors provide an image of the classroom that beginning teachers often cannot see. The challenge for the mentor is to be able to write quickly, concisely, and comprehensively, capturing on paper all that is happening.

Mentors can use several scripting formats to become comfortable with gathering evidence. The adage "Practice makes perfect" also applies to scripting. Mentors can try the following techniques to hone their scripting skills.

- Watch and script talk shows to develop style and shorthand skills.
- Script a conversation that happens at home.
- Sit in on a fellow mentor's class to try out scripting skills.
- Gather with several mentors to observe the same TV show or videotapes of classroom interactions. After everyone scripts, compare each mentor's notes.

Mentors are learning throughout the mentoring process, and their scripting skills will not be fully refined at the beginning of the relationship. Mentors can communicate this to their mentees and ask them to help support the mentor's learning. Their scripts may be less than 100 percent accurate, so they need to ask their mentees to confirm or refute their findings. In this way, each can facilitate the other's growth and development.

The examples to follow offer different scripting methods as well as some sample forms. They represent brief portions of the total script from a lesson.

Anecdotal Record

An anecdotal record (Figure 7.1) is a form of scripting that allows the observer to note events that occur at particular times during the lesson. It includes a place for comments so that interpretations might be captured and set aside for later discussion.

Figure 7.2 shows how an anecdotal record can be used.

The original scripted notes were handwritten on carbon paper forms so that a copy could be given to the mentee during the post-observation conference. This facilitates a more effective post-observation conference, as mentees can read and comment on mentor notes during the conversation. Mentors can also photocopy their notes for mentees. When gathering evidence, mentors usually write out their comments and observations, although a laptop computer also can be used. E-mailing observational notes can also help provide information to the mentee before the post-conference. Shorthand devices, created by the mentor, are frequently used, as Figure 7.2 illustrates. Similar scripting shortcuts are likely to be developed by anyone using scripting to streamline the process. The parentheses in this example contain explanations of shorthand used by the author. The teacher's name also might be shortened to simply a circled *M* (for *Mary,* or a *T* for *teacher*), and student comments indicated by a circled *S*. Because these shorthand techniques are peculiar to each scripter, it is helpful if the

Figure 7.1   Anecdotal Record

Name of Teacher: _____   Date: _____

Name of Mentor: _____   Class/Grade: _____

<u>Time</u>   <u>Anecdotal Notes</u>   <u>Comments</u>

Figure 7.2   Anecdotal Record Example

Name of Teacher:	Ms. Marks	Date: 10-12-99
Name of Mentor:	Mrs. Johnson	Class/Grade: Tenth-Grade Biology

Time	Anecdotal Notes	Comments
8:45	Bell rings Ms. M: "Today we will be looking at the process of photosynthesis. Has anyone heard this term before?" Student: "Yah, it has something to do with the plants being green." Ms. M: "Yes! What else?"	Students are in seats. Ms. M writes student comment on board.
	Students respond.	All student comments are added to list on board; M calls on 5 students—3 g (girls), 2 b (boys). Many students raise their hands, one of the boys called upon did not raise his hand.
9:00	Ms. M: "Okay! Let's take what we already know about this process and add to this info. I'd like you to take out your notebooks and write this down. Jimmy and Julie, notebooks out please."	Overhead of photo. (photosynthesis) process used—nice, clear diagram. J & J (Jimmy and Julie) respond to M's request.
9:15	Ms. M: "Now can anyone think of what this model looks like?" Student: "Some sort of a factory?" Ms. M: "Yes—a factory that produces energy for the plant and oxygen for us!"	Nice use of analogy —students have to think!

mentor is present to interpret any abbreviations and translate any unintelligible handwriting. So, at least for the first postconference, the mentee should be given a copy of the notes only when the mentor is present to clarify the comments.

Freewriting

This technique does not attempt to capture specific statements and observations; it describes the overall sequence of events using a narrative format. Notes are written without use of a particular form or duplicating paper. This written narrative is then shared with the mentee during a post-observation conference. Mentors freely record all that comes into their frame of reference (Figure 7.3). Interpretation that might be included will need to be clarified during the conference. All that is necessary for this technique is a blank sheet of paper and the ability to write continuously throughout the lesson.

Figure 7.3   Freewriting Example

Jack Jones's observation, Tues., March 15, 1997

Fourth grade at HMS elem., 2:00 p.m.

Jack tells the class that they will be starting their literature lesson and asks them to put away the math that they were working on. Students have worksheets on long division on their desks. Some really don't seem to want to put this away, and Jack has to ask them several times to put the math away and get out their copy of the book, *The Cay*. Jack asks one student to tell the class where they should be (page number) and asks students to open books. He begins to read to them. Some students appear to be following along, some seem to be daydreaming. A student raises his hand and asks how Timothy got to the island—says they don't remember that part. Jack asks for a student to give the answer. Many students want to tell this part. A student who is practically jumping up and down is called on and he gives a lengthy description of this part of the story. Jack resumes reading, and then says that students who wish to can volunteer to read one paragraph at a time. Students take turns reading. Jack then asks the students several provocative questions: Why do you think the author had the young boy go blind? What do we think about people who are blind? Is this a stereotype? What can you say about this blind boy? Students get into the discussion, which is teacher-led but seems to involve most students. After this, students are directed to get out their notebooks and write in their literature journals what they think is going to happen next in the novel. Students write until Jack tells them to put their stuff away and get ready to go home.

Jane Smith, observer

Focused Scripting

In this format, mentors use a specific lens to focus their comments. Mentors and mentees should have discussed this lens in the pre-observation conference. Although the lens is always taken into consideration in an observation, focused scripting filters out any potential observations that are not related to it. Other forms of scripting capture all interactions, and the comments are interpreted using the lens during the post-observation conference. In focused scripting, the observer (mentor) looks for evidence in classroom interactions that supports the language and expectations defined in the lens. For example, if the lens used is the INTASC standards, the mentoring program might have developed a form that identifies those standards. The mentor then records occurrences that fit into each category. If there is a specific form, as with the PATHWISE model, this form should be used in a very flexible manner. Rigid adherence to any form limits the perspective that mentors can provide, and the scripting will begin to feel like a summative evaluation rather than the gathering of data about the lesson. However, to avoid overlooking teaching and learning events that are helpful points of discussion, focused scripting can ensure that mentees identify how and where they meet the criteria that is expected of them.

The focused script in Figure 7.4 demonstrates that responses tend to be brief and are focused to correspond to the criteria. In some ways, this form can be helpful to a new scripter, as specific information is being sought. On the other hand, trying to separate the multiple layers of events happening in a classroom and place them into appropriate categories is difficult for beginners. Because classroom interactions do not occur in the order that the principles or criteria are listed on such forms, it is easy for mentors to miss some of what is going on as they search for the right place to record their observations. Mentors who wish to create a scripting form can list the standards and components of the lens they choose and then describe the evidence underneath the related standard. A sample form developed for mentors to use with a frameworks model (Figure 7.5) is provided to show how focused scripting forms might be developed for the various lenses.

Figure 7.4   Focused Scripting Example (Using INTASC Standards)

School District XYZ
Observation Form
Mentee: Becky Martin   Mentor: Heidi Smith
Date: 11/12/97   Class/Grade: Seventh-Grade English

1. Subject Matter
   - Selects teaching methods, activities, and material appropriate for students and the discipline.
   - Demonstrates subject mastery and general teaching knowledge.
   - Understands and teaches the connections between the disciplines, with other disciplines, and with life experiences.

   Evidence:
   Becky describes very clearly her choices for her lesson and her objectives specify the student learning that should occur.

2. Student Learning
   - Demonstrates familiarity with relevant aspects of students' base knowledge and experiences.
   - Demonstrates familiarity with the way students learn and develop.
   - Provides learning opportunities that support students' intellectual, social, and personal growth.

   Evidence:
   Becky said: "Joseph, why don't you and Tommy work together on the ending to the story." All other students were working alone.
   (Note—Becky said later that Joseph didn't work well alone and that she was trying peer teaching.)

3. Diverse Learners
   - Demonstrates familiarity with students' cultural, ethnic, and experiential backgrounds.
   - Demonstrates familiarity with student differences in learning capabilities and approaches.
   - Provides learning opportunities that are adapted for students with diverse backgrounds and exceptionalities.

   Evidence:
   Nothing apparent from lesson—an area to focus on, perhaps?

4. Instructional Strategies
   - Makes the learning goals and instructional procedures clear to students.
   - Makes content comprehensible to students.
   - Encourages students to extend their thinking to include critical thinking, problem solving, and performance skills.

(Continued)

Figure 7.4 (Continued)

Evidence:
Becky had the objectives listed on the board when the students arrived. She identified the vocabulary that she thought would be difficult and had students make educated guesses about the definition (like a game format) and then had them check the definition in the dictionary before reading the story.

5. Learning Environment
   - Creates a climate that promotes fairness and positive social interaction.
   - Communicates behavioral expectations to students and establishes consistent standards of classroom behavior.
   - Attends to making the physical environment safe and conducive to learning.

   Evidence:
   Room is very cheery. Lots of student work on the board. A space is identified where the new endings to the stories students are reading will be displayed upon completion. I wonder if all student work is displayed. Becky works the room and gets around to all students as they work on the story ending. She encourages— "I like that idea"— and refocuses—"Mary, I don't think your math is what you should be doing now."

6. Communication
   - Uses knowledge of effective verbal, nonverbal, and media communication techniques to foster learning.
   - Assists students to communicate effectively about their learning needs and accomplishments.
   - Effectively formulates and asks questions and stimulates discussion.

   Evidence:
   Becky's tone is no-nonsense but not scary. Students are following directions and are on task. Has there been discussion about what they read? Students are directed to their work and they get busy. Later, students read their story endings to each other.

7. Planning Instruction
   - Articulates clear learning goals for the lesson that are appropriate for the students and the content.
   - Selects teaching methods, activities, and materials appropriate for students and content.
   - Plans for instruction; aligns goals, instructions, and evaluation.

   Evidence:
   Lesson plans are clear. Becky will assess the story endings, evaluating reading comprehension, creative writing, and use of adjectives and adverbs in writing to make it more interesting. How will these be evaluated? Is there a rubric?

8. Assessment
   - Demonstrates knowledge of and employs a variety of formal and informal assessment tools.
   - Uses assessment information to adapt instruction and support student learning.
   - Accurately and appropriately reports information regarding student learning.

   Evidence:
   Use of student work as assessment (student writing)—How does this fit into overall evaluation and grading? How is it evaluated?

9. Reflection and Professional Development
   - Reflects on the extent to which the learning goals were met.
   - Demonstrates professional responsibility and integrity.
   - Uses research, colleagues, and professional development opportunities to become a better teacher.

   Evidence:
   Becky is keeping a journal that she says is very helpful when reflecting on what happens in the classroom. She is going to attend a state workshop on adolescent literature next month.

10. Collaboration, Ethics, and Relationships
    - Builds professional relationships with colleagues.
    - Communicates with parents and guardians about student learning.
    - Collaborates with colleagues, families, and the community to foster healthy and productive student development.

    Evidence:
    A newsletter from Becky's class goes home each quarter that includes letters from literature class that contains some excerpts from student work and specifies the main objectives for each quarter. She talks about her desire to get to know the other seventh-grade teachers better—a goal will be to make that happen.

Figure 7.5   Focused Observation Guide Using the Frameworks Model

District XYZ

Name _____   Date _____

Elements preceded by (1) should be an area of primary focus for 1st-year mentees

Components of Planning & Preparation	*The Classroom Environment*
• Demonstrating knowledge of content & pedagogy • Demonstrating knowledge of students • **(1)** Selecting instructional goals Demonstrating knowledge of resources • **(1)** Designing coherent instruction • Assessing student learning	• **(1)** Creating an environment of respect & rapport • Creating a culture for learning • **(1)** Managing classroom procedures • **(1)** Managing student behavior • Organizing physical space

Instruction	*Professional Responsibilities*
• **(1)** Communicating clearly & accurately • Use of questions & discussion techniques • **(1)** Engaging students • **(1)** Providing feedback to students • Being flexible & responsive	• Reflecting • **(1)** Record-keeping • **(1)** Communication with families • Contributing to school & district • Allowing for professional growth & development • Maintaining professionalism

Visual/Auditory Evidence (I Saw . . . I Heard . . . I Thought . . .)

In Chapter 3, an observation form (Figure 3.3) was provided that asked mentors to write down only what they saw and heard and to specifically record one positive area as well as one area of concern. This form was to be used by the mentor to generate guiding questions to facilitate discussion. While it may not capture the full extent of classroom interactions, it is a good way for mentors to begin gathering evidence while limiting evaluative or judgmental comments. This version is simple and very open-ended and thus less intimidating for both parties; mentors can increase their skills without having to note so many interactions, and mentees are not overwhelmed by so much data.

In addition to the example in Figure 3.3, another simplified form (Figure 7.6) can assist mentors in capturing just what is seen and heard in the classroom without editorializing. This simpler form allows mentors even more flexibility in gathering data, but it assumes there will be a post-observation conference in which mentees can comment further on the notes. A lens could also be used as a part of the interpretation of these observations during discussions.

Figure 7.6   Observation Notes

Mentor: _____	Date: _____
Mentee: _____	Class/Grade: _____

When watching your class

I saw . . .	*I heard . . .*	*I thought . . .*

Figure 7.7   Example of Observation Notes

I saw . . .	*I heard . . .*	*I thought . . .*
Becky (the teacher) watched the class start working on the assignment. She then went over to two boys and spoke to them. She then moved the boys closer together.	Becky said, "Why don't you [Joseph] and Tommy work together on the ending to the story?"	I wondered if either of these boys was struggling, and perhaps Becky put them together so that one could help the other. I wondered what the other kids would think about two students getting to work together when all of the rest had to work alone.

Applied to the same lesson taught by Becky described in Figure 7.4, the comments captured on this form regarding student learning might look like the example provided in Figure 7.7.

Using this simple format, mentors capture only what is actually seen and heard, but they are able to jot down any unknowns or questions in the *I thought* column. This allows for further clarification when the notes are discussed with the mentee. In this way, mentors are not making a judgment about the event but are opening the door to further conversation. The *I thought* section enables mentees to think about the interaction from the mentors' perspective, and also enables them to respond and to talk about why an event occurred. For example, Becky might have put the boys together because they always talked and, by doing so, given them permission for what was going to occur. If this were the case, the mentor's question about the feelings of the other children would be valid. However, if Becky put the two boys together to offer support for a struggling learner, she has shown insight into the needs of her students and is making this choice to support their learning. In either case, the mentor does not know what is true. If mentors jot down their thoughts as they see and hear something occur in the classroom, they can ask questions later to fully explore the reasons behind the classroom interactions.

■ PROXIMITY ANALYSIS

Sometimes a picture is worth a thousand words when a mentor is trying to reflect what is happening in a classroom. Conducting a proximity

Dialogue: Various Scripting Formats

Look over the examples provided in Figures 7.1 to 7.7 and consider which one you might start with as you script your classroom observations.

- Discuss with another mentor your response to each format and give reasons for your choice. What are the strengths and weaknesses of each format?
- Identify why you might use a different format for different mentees or situations.
- Identify what the information scripted in each example tells you about the lesson.
- Discuss how you might approach your post-observation conference using this data.

analysis can supply novice teachers with an image of their movements around the classroom and among students. This diagram can help make beginning teachers aware of which students they are focusing on and which they are not paying as much attention to in the classroom. A proximity analysis can also demonstrate to teachers how comfortable they are getting up close and personal with their students. However, before creating a proximity analysis, mentors should ask their mentees if they want another picture of their work in the classroom. Glickman et al. (1997) identify the importance of both the mentor and mentee's involvement when determining what type of information would be most helpful to the novice teacher. If the novice is comfortable with this format, the mentor should proceed. However, if the mentee is uncomfortable, it would be best to wait and conduct the analysis later in their relationship, or to explain further why this type of data would be helpful.

The use of proximity has long been considered an aid in classroom management. Most students are less likely to be off task if the teacher is standing right next to them. A description of proximity identifies which students are getting the teacher's attention—whether for academic support or for maintaining positive behavior. During the post-observation conference, mentees can address why they moved closer to some students and did not engage others. This reflection enables novice teachers to identify the reasons for their behavior and to attune themselves to their movements in the classroom.

A diagram of the classroom is a helpful tool in starting a proximity analysis. If the teacher has a seating chart, the mentor can simply make a copy and draw on it. If no such map is available, a quick sketch of the seating arrangement will do. The drawing should identify key areas: chalkboard, teacher's desk, and student seating. A legend should be included to identify codes used to indicate people or actions in the design. The goal of a proximity analysis is to capture the teacher's movement in the classroom, indicated by an arrow and/or line. The mentor can include an indicator of teacher movement during the lesson by numbering the

Figure 7.8   Proximity Analysis

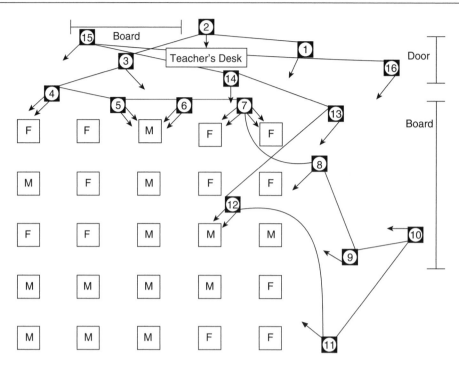

KEY: Circle represents teacher's stops in movement
A double arrow represents teacher talking directly to one student
A single arrow represents teacher talking to the whole class
M = male, F = female

stops he or she makes or perhaps by noting the duration of each pause in his or her movement. In addition, the mentor can note any other pertinent information—such as where the teacher is directing his or her comments—by drawing arrows or using some other symbol. There are no absolutes in creating a proximity diagram, except that the completed diagram should identify where the teacher was at particular moments throughout the lesson. Figure 7.8 demonstrates one way to create a proximity analysis.

Mentees need to put the proximity analysis into context during a debriefing conversation with their mentors in the post-observation conference. Without the debriefing conversation, any proximity diagram reflects only half of the story. For example, perhaps the teacher purposefully avoided a section of the room because students there always call out for attention, or perhaps she directed several comments toward one child because that student was absent yesterday and needed additional help.

The exercise on page 97 asks mentors to reflect on the proximity analysis in Figure 7.8 to get practice interpreting a proximity analysis.

This proximity chart shows that the teacher's movements keep him or her primarily at the front of the room or by the side of the chalkboard. At first glance, it could be interpreted that the teacher is ignoring the half of the class that is in the back of the room, away from the chalkboard. It also could be speculated that the teacher is connecting with a large number of the students. Without asking questions, mentors will not know what is true. Mentors might start out by saying, "I diagrammed your movements

Dialogue: Proximity Analysis

DIALOGUE

After you review Figure 7.8 for a few minutes, consider what the diagram says to you. Consider how you would discuss this with your mentee. What patterns do you see that might need further explanation? What questions should you ask? Think about how you might begin a conversation with a mentee as you share this data. In addition, identify what misconceptions might be created without the mentee's interpretation of this diagram. Now practice this by role-playing with a colleague, or by writing out the questions you would ask and the comments you would make. Sharing an interpretation with a colleague can validate your interpretation or help you to rethink your analysis of the diagram.

while you were teaching, as we had discussed, and I wonder what you think about this." In this case, hopefully, the mentee would notice the disproportionate use of the classroom space and offer a response. If not, mentors can offer their thoughts. It could be that the mentee was providing extra help and support to those students he or she moved close to and the other students were functioning quite well on their own. Or perhaps the novice teacher was intimidated by the students in the back (who are mostly males) and was avoiding them, or he or she was totally unaware that the classroom space was not being used very effectively.

The discussion of the data gathered through the proximity analysis provides increased awareness for mentees and offers opportunities for them to make changes in their teaching. The benefit of this thinking-out-loud kind of dialogue is that mentors are able to extend the conversation and support the novice teacher's thinking by providing another view of classroom interactions. It is not always easy for mentors to facilitate effective conversations with their mentees, but specific data, like that gathered in a proximity analysis, provide a clear starting point.

VERBAL FLOW ■

Diagramming the flow of teacher talk during a lesson can be the sole focus of an observation. While a proximity diagram can include some indicators identifying to whom the teacher is talking, it is challenging to simultaneously gather the movements of the novice teacher and to identify the verbal interactions during the same observation. Looking solely at the verbal flow in the classroom allows mentors to gather evidence about how teachers and students engage in conversation during a lesson. This is an especially useful tool to use during class discussions, when mentees are working to involve all students in the conversation.

A diagram of the verbal flow helps teachers see which individuals received most of their comments, who was being called on, and how much of the conversation was directed by the teacher or particular students. It is helpful for mentors to start with a seating chart, or they can sketch a quick diagram of the classroom. During the discussion, mentors

Figure 7.9   Verbal-Flow Diagram

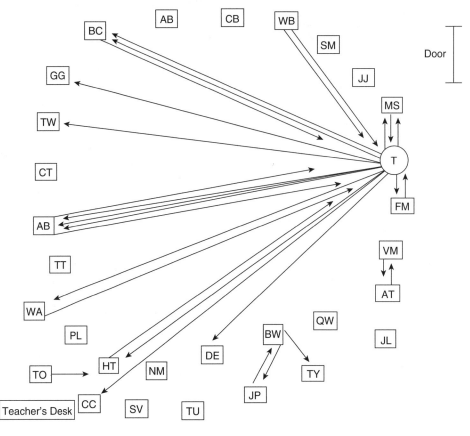

KEY: T in circle = teacher
     Student initials in square = name of student
     Arrows point out the direction of the communication flow

simply draw arrows to indicate who is speaking to whom. They can script some of the discussion that corresponds to the verbal-flow diagram to capture the type of questions posed by the teacher and the responses made by students, as well as the teacher's follow-up. Comments may be difficult to include in the verbal-flow diagram, but if mentors diagram part of the discussion and script another part of it, they can compile some interesting data.

Indicating the amount of classroom time covered by the verbal-flow diagram can also help teachers see how much time certain interactions required. Again, it is important that mentees have an opportunity to provide context to the diagram during the post-observation conference so any underlying decisions made by the novice teacher during the lesson are made clear to mentors.

Figure 7.9 is an example of a verbal-flow diagram.

A mentor's discussion of the verbal-flow diagram might focus on a number of things. The conversation could be started by simply sharing the diagram and asking the mentee what he or she thinks about it. The mentee might recognize that most comments during class seemed to be directed

Dialogue: Verbal Flow

Consider what the data in the verbal-flow diagram (Figure 7.9) seem to indicate. With another mentor, identify some reasons why this verbal flow might reflect a desired interaction during a class discussion, and why it might reflect some undesired interactions. It might be helpful to practice verbalizing your thoughts regarding the verbal-flow diagram, as if you were talking directly to your mentee.

toward a few students and that some were never engaged in any discussions. He may notice that some students seemed to be having side conversations. This can lead to a discussion about why some students may be talking with the teacher more often and what kinds of strategies could encourage all students to participate. Small-group discussions and cooperative learning might be some strategies the mentor can recommend. Perhaps the students who were involved in the conversation had some questions that needed further explanation. Perhaps the side conversations were off task or perhaps these students were simply asking to borrow a pencil. The mentee needs to reflect on why this series of verbal interactions took place and determine what needs to be done to strengthen them. The verbal-flow diagram provides data on one lesson's conversations. The discussion of these issues is the most valuable aspect of this process.

NUMERIC DATA

Scripting and the use of diagrams provide evidence of classroom interactions that are qualitative and descriptive. Sometimes it is helpful for mentees to receive more quantitative data. Counting the types of questions or the number of reprimands in a class period can be helpful information, depending on the novice teacher's goals. Again, mentors should discuss using a particular data-gathering device with mentees during the pre-observation conference, so they are not surprised by what is presented to them during the post-observation discussion.

For example, if mentees are using a particular idiom or interjection in their speech that might be distracting to learners, it might be helpful for mentors to count how often they occurred to provide mentees with evidence that the speech pattern is not a random occurrence. "You guys," "like," "you know" and "um" are examples of often-unconscious interjections used by novice teachers. While mentees may not be able to totally eliminate these phrases from their speech, being aware of the number of times they are used can help new teachers concentrate on more effective language. These data can also be helpful as a starting point when creating an action plan to focus on alternative language choices.

Numeric data can also be used to identify occurrences of student behavior. A time chart used to identify the number of students who appear to be off task at intervals throughout the lesson is one such format. A chart listing categories of questions might be used to keep track of how many higher-level questions teachers use in a lesson, or perhaps to count the types of comments teachers make. For example, a list of items could be created including categories such as asking questions, giving directions, reprimanding and encouraging students, and a check mark made every time novice teachers make such a comment.

Numeric evidence, which provides hard data, can appear to be less supportive than other forms of data gathering. That is why it is important that mentors confer with mentees first. This tool is often helpful when mentees are not able to see what they are doing when provided with scripted evidence. Mentors may then need to be more directive, and numeric data can provide support for directive comments. For example, if a novice teacher is aware of the need to ask open-ended questions to involve students in a discussion but continues to ask yes/no questions despite scripted evidence of that tendency, it might be helpful to count the types of questions being asked. With numeric data, mentors can indicate that a certain activity is occurring too frequently or not often enough and that the mentee needs to reduce or increase these occurrences. However, it is important that these data be given only to the mentee and kept confidential.

The dialogue on the next page allows mentors to reflect on using numeric data when observing their mentees.

Mentors might wonder when it is appropriate to use numeric data. Or they might be concerned that the gathering of such quantified evidence does not address the human side of the teaching act. Some of them, when discussing this issue, have commented that when the number of times someone does something is counted, the tally can seem to validate or refute an issue. Thus, the use of numeric data needs to be focused on some aspect of the mentee's teaching that can be, and should be, counted.

For example, if the intent is to determine the number of times open-ended questions are asked, numeric data will identify this information. However, these data do not reflect all the other interactions that occurred during the lesson. Mentors need to think about whether the numeric data are being gathered to point out how poorly questions are being asked or to show that, indeed, some questions are very good. If mentees do not see that they are asking only lower-order questions, a count of the number of open-ended questions will certainly point that out. More important, however, is that mentees develop the awareness that they need to be asking open-ended questions. The interpretation of the data can support a mentee's efforts or point out that they are not effective. However, it is the scripting of some of the questions and of students' responses to them that may provide more support for the mentee's ongoing use of a particular questioning format.

Above all, mentors need to be very clear about what they want to accomplish when gathering numeric data. Numeric data-gathering should be used very intentionally and should be discussed carefully with the mentee so that the data support ongoing learning. If a mentee feels that the data are being gathered simply to point out his or her poor efforts, the damage in the relationship with the mentor will be irreparable.

■ VIDEO- AND AUDIOTAPING

A videotape of a lesson provides the ultimate mirror image of the classroom. The tape captures everything going on in the classroom (within

Dialogue: Use of Numeric Data

DIALOGUE

With another mentor, discuss your comfort level with the use of numeric data, or think about the issues contained in the following questions:

1. When would you gather this type of evidence?
2. How might the use of numeric data impact your relationship with your mentee?

range) and can help a 1st-year teacher see very explicitly what is happening. Although mentors may not notice all that goes on during a lesson or may select only certain pieces of evidence to share with their mentees, the video camera records everything. Consequently, mentors must use caution when taping beginning teachers, as novices can be easily overwhelmed by all that they see on tape. In most cases, mentors should consider waiting until later in the year before videotaping a beginning teacher. However, if mentees are having difficulty identifying how their lessons are going or seem unable to reflect on their work, a videotape can provide the concrete evidence needed to help them see their teaching more clearly.

It is typical for novice teachers watching a video of themselves to focus more on their own self-image and not completely see all the teaching and learning events. This is especially true for beginning teachers who may still be narrowly focused on themselves and who do not yet have a broader vision of the classroom. However, it also can be helpful for mentees to tape themselves early in the fall and then again later in the spring to demonstrate growth over the course of the year. Due to the distraction that a camera can create in a classroom, mentors should operate the camera and facilitate the taping. A strategy that works well is to set up the camera early in the year and leave it in the classroom so students become used to having it around. Then, when the camera is discreetly turned on, students will not digress into camera-crazy behavior. Be sure the videos are erased after viewing, unless you get permission from the videotaped students and mentee.

If the goal is to gather evidence about a mentee's verbal interactions, the mentor can use an audiotape as a less obtrusive method rather than videotaping. Whether using an audiotape or videotape, mentors should watch or listen to the recording with their mentees to provide alternative viewpoints, especially if the mentee tends to focus on the negative aspects of his or her work. The mentor's perspective provides valuable balance.

It is critical that mentors develop a range of data-gathering skills to enhance the conversations they have with mentees. Mentors need to plan and hone their observational skills so they avoid a random approach to classroom observations and provide helpful information (Moir & Bloom, 2003). Use of the data-gathering tools and techniques identified in this chapter can help mentors support novice teachers as they work to improve their skills.

8

Evaluating the Mentoring Experience

Novice teachers are sometimes thrust into teaching with little training. They are often given the most difficult classes as well as additional duties, such as coaching assignments or study hall supervision. They are frequently left in isolated classrooms to fend for themselves, leaving them feeling alone, frustrated, and bereft of support. The combination of faculty members' busy schedules and novice teachers' feelings of fear about sharing their needs often results in their concerns going unnoticed. The responsibility of providing support to new teachers is often left up to a few interested or selected individuals.

Beginning teachers fare best when the whole school community is committed to their ongoing growth and development. In order for the teaching profession to flourish and continue to provide appropriate and effective learning opportunities for students, new teachers must be supported (Johnson, 2004). While mentoring programs often provide specific means by which to do so, some educators suggest that experienced teachers must be careful not to limit other, more informal, mentoring opportunities. "Whether through chance meetings in hallways or scheduled discussions during planning periods, as experienced teachers we must all do all we can to stop the feelings of failure that new teachers inevitably experience" (Delgado, 1999, p. 29). Identified mentors may provide the main support for beginning teachers, but the village elders of a school community must contribute as well.

Individual teachers or groups of teachers who have decided to work with novices understand that mentoring requires preparation beyond the skills they use in their own classrooms. According to the

National Commission on Teaching and America's Future (2000), mentoring programs need to provide mentors with appropriate information, training, practice, and support. These programs can be configured in many different ways. However, in those that are successful, the time needed for mentoring and ways for mentors and mentees to get together within their busy school schedules are carefully considered (Brooks, 2000).

Mentors also must have the opportunity to reflect on their work and to conduct a dialogue with others in similar positions to expand their knowledge and effectiveness. Their training is critical (Giebelhaus & Bowman, 2000). Although mentors may be taking part in activities designed to increase their effectiveness, they may still wonder to what degree they are affecting their mentees' growth. This is hard to measure, but certain techniques and tools can be employed to help mentors appraise their effectiveness.

■ PROGRAM EVALUATION

Evaluating mentoring programs and the work of individual mentors is helpful in determining whether sufficient support is being provided to novice teachers. It is important to ascertain whether mentors are competent and comfortable with their role and whether mentees are receiving the support they need to be successful. Positive results are reflected in the retention rate of new teachers and by the degree to which supervisors/administrators feel comfortable with the novice teachers' work (Evertson & Smithey, 2000; Johnson et al., 2003). However, these measures of effectiveness are very broad and do not identify other factors that may impact the success of the novice. Therefore, a formal evaluation that seeks information regarding the beginning teacher's increased effectiveness and the perceived impact of the mentor on the novice's learning is very helpful. Evaluation supports mentoring programs by identifying areas of strength and those in which the process could be improved.

As discussed in earlier chapters, although evaluations can be beneficial, it is strongly recommended that mentors do not evaluate novice teachers (Feiman-Nemser et al., 1999). If mentors become evaluators, mentees will fear that their requests for help or discussion of problems will be documented in an evaluation rather than being used as a starting point for ongoing learning. This impacts and limits the effectiveness of a mentoring program.

Regardless of these concerns, mentors have taken on the role of evaluator in some programs. Done in the right way, this can be helpful to the new teacher, although the mentoring relationship will be quite different. For example, the California Formative Assessment and Support System for Teachers (CFASST) is a program that includes a formative assessment given by mentors. This model provides opportunities for beginning teachers and their support providers to "engage in structured assessment tasks over a two-year period" (Olebe, Jackson, & Danielson, 1999, p. 42). This type of structured assessment may be a viable option as it allows both mentor and mentee to engage in predefined tasks that clearly evaluate their roles and responsibilities. It is possible to design a program that includes assessment by the mentor, but the assessment needs to be carefully structured and incorporate formative evaluation. In the CFASST model, the purpose of the assessment is not formal teacher evaluation. Rather, a common set of scales or "descriptions of practice" based on Charlotte Danielson's work is used to describe teaching practice at different levels (Obele et al., 1999).

The success of a beginning teacher can reflect the success of a mentoring program. Therefore, it might be tempting to simply evaluate beginning teachers using the district model for retention of teachers or to determine that a mentoring program was successful if the students in the novice teacher's classroom met achievement goals. However, this does not help to improve programs. To examine the effectiveness of a mentoring program, mentees need to be asked what the process did for them. The impact of mentoring may go beyond the scope of what is seen in the classroom during an observation and may be much more comprehensive than the data compiled through the use of a rating scale.

Whether the mentee received informal mentoring or was involved in an organized program, the effectiveness of the mentoring is best identified by those directly affected. An evaluation that asks open-ended questions to gather information about the mentee's perceptions of the mentoring program offers the most complete view.

The use of a questionnaire, such as the example shown in Figure 8.1, provides quantitative evidence regarding the impact of the program and provides suggestions for increasing its effectiveness. It is best if someone besides the mentor—such as the building principal or staff development director—administers the evaluation. In any case, mentees should be encouraged to be honest with their feedback.

An evaluation tool, such as this mentor evaluation form, identifies the mentee's perceptions. It is also important that a mentorship director, if there is one, gather information from the others involved in the mentoring relationship—the supervisors and the mentors—to get a three-dimensional look at the program.

The questions shown in Figure 8.2 can be answered by mentors to provide themselves and mentoring program directors with some feedback and evaluation regarding their role in the process. Mentors, directors of mentoring programs, or other district administrators can give the evaluation questions in Figure 8.3 to supervisors. As the third party of the mentoring relationship, supervisors can often offer an unbiased view of the mentoring process.

Once this information has been gathered from all three sources, mentors or the director of the mentoring program should categorize the data and note patterns. These data should make clear what worked and what needs to be refined. If specific information is needed to shape a program, questions can be added to the survey. For example, if a mentoring program matched mentors and mentees based on certain criteria, then both need to be asked if they felt this match was effective and helpful (Garvey, 1999). If a program does not specifically match mentors and mentees, then a question pertaining to matching is not helpful. On the other hand, if a program is considering matching mentors and mentees, a question that directs mentees and mentors to consider their preference for working with someone with a similar philosophy or personality is appropriate.

Figure 8.1   Mentee Evaluation of the Program

Consider the support you received from your mentor this year in answering the following:

1. During the past year, what did your mentor do that was most beneficial for you?

2. During the past year, what did your mentor do that was the least beneficial for you?

3. List specific areas of your teaching where your mentor provided support.

4. List several ways in which your mentor provided the support you listed in question 3.

5. In what other ways did your mentor meet your needs during the first year?

6. Were you given sufficient time to work with your mentor? How could your time together be improved?

7. What would you like to see added to the mentoring program for next year's 1st-year teachers?

Figure 8.2   Mentor Evaluation of the Program

1. What do you think was the most valuable aspect of mentoring for your mentee?

2. What was the most valuable aspect of mentoring for you?

3. What aspect(s) of mentoring did you find most difficult?

4. List the specific areas/topics that you worked on with your mentee.

5. Did you have sufficient time to work with your mentee? How could your time together be improved?

6. What would you like to see added to the mentoring program for next year's novice teachers?

7. What kinds of support and/or training would you like to see provided to new mentors beyond what you were given?

8. List any additional information that you think would be helpful for future mentors to be aware of as they work with mentees.

Figure 8.3   Supervisor Evaluation of the Program

1. What do you think was the most valuable aspect of mentoring for the mentee you evaluated?

2. As a supervisor, what was the most valuable aspect of mentoring for you?

3. Did you see improvement on the part of the novice teacher that you attribute to mentoring? If so, list the areas of improvement.

4. What aspect of mentoring do you feel was the most valuable for the *mentee?* Why?

5. What aspect of mentoring do you feel was the most valuable for the *mentor?* Why?

6. What resources did you provide to the mentor to support his or her work? (List monetary compensation, resources, time, materials, training, etc.) Would you change that for next year? Why or why not?

7. Other comments, concerns, or questions?

Supervisors have an additional tool that can help to identify the effectiveness of mentoring. Usually evaluators/supervisors formally observe beginning teachers early in the year. Supervisors can then compare this observation with one conducted later in the school year. They should note improvements and compare this data with the surveys completed by mentees and mentors. If an area addressed by the mentor and mentee is also an area in which the supervisor noted improvement between the first formal observation and the second, some of that growth can be attributed to the mentoring process.

Since the growth and development of novice teachers is the ultimate goal of the mentoring process, supervisors should look closely at mentees' overall effectiveness. If they end their first year in the classroom with stronger skills and methods for effectively supporting student learning, then the goal was met. Identifying how much of the novice's effectiveness can be attributed to mentoring is not an exact science. However, by conducting surveys and looking at a mentee's growth over time, supervisors can identify some of the program's impact. This comparison should in no way compromise the confidentiality of the mentoring relationship, but it should serve as another way to view the effectiveness of the program.

EVALUATION FOR PERSONAL GROWTH: MENTORS

As mentors work to interact more effectively with novice teachers, it is helpful for them to identify areas for their own personal growth. They might want some suggestions about how to use questioning or verbal skills more effectively. Asking a trained colleague to sit in on a mentoring session and provide feedback is one way to identify areas of strength as well as areas where more development is needed. While this may seem like an awkward situation, a partner-mentor is valuable because she can provide feedback from a similar perspective. Someone who has never been a mentor will not have the same vantage point. This type of observation should only be conducted after the mentor and mentee have firmly established their relationship.

In addition, informal surveys of mentees can be used to identify areas where mentors might want to focus their own development. Because of the personal nature of these surveys, it is helpful if another individual, such as the supervisor or the director of the mentoring program, gathers data anonymously so that mentees can be assured that their comments will not adversely affect their relationship with their mentors. For example, a supervisor could issue the survey to the mentee and then provide feedback to the mentor in a general format. This type of feedback works best in programs where a mentor works with several mentees to provide a greater level of anonymity for the mentee. In one-on-one mentoring programs, it is difficult to collect data anonymously. Mentees who are providing suggestions or comments may be more honest if they are not asked to evaluate early in the mentoring relationship. Regardless of the length of a program, information should be gathered at the end of the first year of mentoring so that mentors can focus on the identified skills the following year. Figure 8.4 is an example of a form that can be given to mentees by a supervisor to discern areas where mentors might want to focus their growth.

Another way for individual mentors to determine their level of growth is to look at the difference between their knowledge base before and after taking part in a preparation program. For example, mentors can complete a survey of their skills and knowledge base prior to reading this text and taking part in the dialoguing exercises. After completing the book, mentors can take the survey again to measure growth. While self-reporting is not completely accurate, the pre- and post-test questionnaires (Figures 8.5 and 8.6) give mentors, or those facilitating a mentoring preparation program, a means of determining if awareness increased after training programs (like reading and participating in the ideas presented in this text). These questionnaires can provide mentors with the information they need to enhance the growth and development of their mentoring skills.

■ EVALUATION FOR PERSONAL GROWTH: THE NOVICE TEACHER

Portfolio

Beginning teachers need to take ownership for gathering their own evidence of their growth as teachers. The use of a portfolio to document lesson plans, creative units, and classroom management plans can be very helpful. In addition, reflective documents in a portfolio provide evidence of a mentee's ability to problem-solve and reflect on what she has learned. A notebook or an electronic portfolio gives novice teachers a place to keep track of their work for later reference and support. Mentors should encourage mentees to keep a portfolio and should offer to review it and provide feedback about the contents and organization of the materials. This portfolio might be used as a part of an evaluation conference or a future job search, so mentees should be strongly encouraged to develop one that meets their needs. In addition, mentors can also develop a portfolio to identify their own learning that has resulted from their work with mentees. This professional project can enhance mentors' reflection skills.

Mentors might suggest that mentees keep sample lesson plans that demonstrate the range of their pedagogical skills as well as any notes from teachers and parents, unit plans, and other curriculum materials they developed for inclusion in the portfolio. A description of their classroom management plans and their goals for continued professional development also might be a part of the portfolio. Observation reports might be included as evidence of the mentee's willingness to receive and act upon feedback. In addition, the mentee's reflections, written after lessons or after conversations with the mentor, can be included as evidence of an ability to problem-solve and to monitor and adjust teaching practices.

The portfolio is a record of the growth and development of the mentee. As a partner in the novice teacher's ongoing learning, mentors can use the portfolio as evidence of the efforts the mentee has made to continue to develop. Discussing what the mentee selects for inclusion in the portfolio also can serve as a means to identify goals for the mentee as well as to

Figure 8.4   Mentoring Feedback Form

(To be completed by the mentee)

Name of mentor: _____

Communication Skills:

Please rank your mentor's ability to clearly articulate his or her ideas and suggestions to you.

1   2   3   4   5   6   7   8   9   10

misunderstandings   easily understood,
occurred often   specific, clear language

Questioning Skills:

Please rank your mentor's ability to ask questions that enable you to think critically about your teaching.

1   2   3   4   5   6   7   8   9   10

few questions;   questions make me think
tells me what to do   about why/how I make a decision

Knowledge/Resources:

Please rank your mentor's ability to provide you with ideas and resources.

1   2   3   4   5   6   7   8   9   10

few ideas   multiple resources and
or suggestions   suggestions when I
when I ask   need them

Support:

Please rank your mentor's ability to provide you with support, both academic and nonacademic.

1   2   3   4   5   6   7   8   9   10

little support   met all my needs

Please list any additional information regarding this mentor's work that you think would be helpful to him or her for developing mentoring skills.

Figure 8.5   Mentor-Teacher Questionnaire 1

(Complete *prior* to reading *Mentoring Novice Teachers: Fostering a Dialogue Process.*)

Please circle the number corresponding to your knowledge and/or skill. (A rating of 1 indicates little or no expertise; a 5 indicates significant ability or knowledge.)

	(low)				(high)
1. Understanding of the roles of the mentor-teacher, mentee, and supervisor	1	2	3	4	5
2. Understanding of the needs of the beginning teacher	1	2	3	4	5
3. Communication skills:					
trust building	1	2	3	4	5
verbal skills	1	2	3	4	5
nonverbal skills	1	2	3	4	5
4. Conferencing skills:					
use of guiding questions	1	2	3	4	5
listening skills	1	2	3	4	5
5. Data gathering during observations:					
scripting	1	2	3	4	5
other techniques (please list):					
_____	1	2	3	4	5
_____	1	2	3	4	5
_____	1	2	3	4	5
_____	1	2	3	4	5
_____	1	2	3	4	5
6. Use of model (lens) while observing (e.g., PATHWISE, Danielson's framework)					
Name of lens: _____	1	2	3	4	5
7. Use of action plan and goal setting to focus learning	1	2	3	4	5

Figure 8.6   Mentor-Teacher Questionnaire 2

(Complete after reading *Mentoring Novice Teachers: Fostering a Dialogue Process.*)

Please circle the number corresponding to your knowledge and/or skill. (A rating of 1 indicates little or no expertise; a 5 indicates significant ability or knowledge.)

	(low)				(high)
1. Understanding of the roles of the mentor-teacher, mentee, and supervisor	1	2	3	4	5
2. Understanding of the needs of the beginning teacher	1	2	3	4	5
3. Communication skills:					
trust building	1	2	3	4	5
verbal skills	1	2	3	4	5
nonverbal skills	1	2	3	4	5
4. Conferencing skills:					
use of guiding questions	1	2	3	4	5
listening skills	1	2	3	4	5
5. Data gathering during observations:					
scripting	1	2	3	4	5
other techniques (please list):					
_____	1	2	3	4	5
_____	1	2	3	4	5
_____	1	2	3	4	5
_____	1	2	3	4	5
_____	1	2	3	4	5
6. Use of model (lens) while observing (e.g., PATHWISE, Danielson's framework)					
Name of lens:_____	1	2	3	4	5
7. Use of action plan and goal setting to focus learning	1	2	3	4	5

highlight strengths. In any case, a collection of lessons, management plans, and other documents that demonstrate progress provide a holistic view of the mentee's work. The richness, or lack thereof, of the selections and reflections included in the portfolio provides clear evidence of teacher growth.

Letters of Recommendation

New teachers, eager to add to their portfolio or placement file, may ask their mentors to write them letters of recommendation. This request should not be construed as a signal that the mentee is looking for a new job. Rather, the letter can be a significant means of support when, and if, the novice teacher seeks a new position. A letter of recommendation is not an evaluation. It is a description of the mentee's work and development during the year. Who can better describe that growth than someone who has been a part of the learning experience? When writing a letter of recommendation, mentors need to consider their use of language. Administrators often use letters of recommendation to help them decide who will be asked to a job interview, so the wording in this document needs to be carefully crafted.

Letters of recommendation from mentors carry significant weight in the eyes of educational leaders. Teachers and administrators involved in the hiring process want to hear what another teacher—one who worked closely with the novice educator—has to say. Teachers and administrators look to the letter from the mentor for an honest description of a potential faculty member's ability. If mentees do not request such a letter for their files, mentors might suggest to their mentees that such a letter might be useful in providing potential future employers with additional information.

However, mentors need to consider that writing a letter of recommendation often veers into the realm of evaluation. Mentors are being asked to recommend their mentees for a potential job, and thus the language used needs to be carefully chosen. Mentors should keep a few suggestions in mind when writing a letter of recommendation. A letter of recommendation should do the following:

• Signal the level of a mentor's support and identify the mentee's one main strength in the opening statement. The rest of the letter should provide evidence that supports this strength. "Thomas has been my mentee for the past year, and I have been so impressed by his ability to engage his seventh-grade history students in higher-level thinking."

• Identify the mentor's position (relative to the mentee) and the grade and/or content the mentee teaches in the first few sentences.

• Provide subcategories of the mentee's strengths that support the opening ideas. These can form the basis for the paragraphs within the letter. The key areas, domains, or components of the observational lens should be used as the focus for each supporting paragraph so that the mentor does not inadvertently send a red flag by omitting any mention of important areas, such as classroom management. "Thomas uses student-centered strategies; his assessments are always appropriate, and his energy and enthusiasm make the classroom a productive and well-managed learning environment that is also fun for his students." (Following this sentence should be one paragraph describing Thomas's student-centered strategies, one outlining his assessments, and one defining his energy level and enthusiasm. This information forms the body of the letter.)

- Provide evidence and specific examples to support all statements. The mentor needs to avoid statements that might be ambiguous or misleading. "Students were divided into learning groups and given a choice of options for their projects." (This statement supports the presence of student-centered strategies cited above.)

- Include a statement about classroom management. This can be incorporated into comments on any of the subcategories or it can be included in a section by itself. (This topic is a key area of interest for those hiring new teachers.) "Using games and role-playing as assessment techniques can create management issues, but Thomas structured these activities to keep the focus on learning."

- Use positive, supportive language, but identify areas for growth, so the letter is believable. (Some suggest that written letters of recommendation need to include the candidates' weaknesses. Describing these as areas where the novice teacher has worked to improve acknowledges that these areas are challenging but also points out that the mentee has made an effort to address these concerns.) "While some beginning teachers give up when active learning gets a bit out of hand, Thomas worked to develop greater levels of structure so his students were able to meet the predetermined objectives."

- Be professional. The mentor should use district stationery and include his or her title with the signature. The mentor should also carefully proofread the letter.

- Include anything that the mentee specifically wants to have included in the letter. The mentor may also allow the mentee to view the letter. (The letter will probably be placed into the mentee's portfolio or placement file, and the mentee has access to these.)

- Close with a statement that qualifies the mentor's recommendation. "I highly recommend Thomas for any position in the area of social studies." (*Highly* is the qualifier in this statement.)

- Be succinct—one page, two at the most. Most administrators may be pressed for time and appreciate a letter that is direct and to the point.

- Include a phone number and indicate that the mentor is available to provide more in-depth comments.

- Duplicate the letter for the mentor's files. Future employers may call for further information, and mentors may need a copy of the letter to reread and refresh their memory.

There may be times when a mentor has reservations about the mentee and is unsure about how to write a letter that honestly conveys these concerns without eliminating the novice from consideration for possible job opportunities. Mentors can incorporate some red flags into their letter so that administrators can read between the lines and make their own judgments about the candidate. It is important that mentors not write anything that is unsubstantiated or may be considered defamation of character. Mentors need to keep in mind that novice teachers who really struggle in their first teaching experience can, over time, work through issues and develop into competent, effective educators. However, it is equally important that mentors convey concerns—especially those in areas that might not be easily remedied. The suggestions below can help mentors determine appropriate ways to incorporate these concerns into their letters of recommendation. A letter of recommendation may do the following:

- Omit a key area. For example, not mentioning classroom management could be a red flag.

- Describe an area in which a mentee has made progress. "Thomas has steadily improved in his ability to connect his objective to the lesson."

- Indicate the need for ongoing learning and improvement (when this is beyond the norm for most beginners). "With continued support and effort, Thomas will undoubtedly increase his ability to effectively evaluate student learning" or "With strong support from a district mentoring program, Thomas will continue to grow as an educator."

- Describe activities in which the mentee has participated, but include no descriptors. "Thomas taught several sections of seventh-grade history, writing lesson plans and conducting the class activities for several weeks." (No further mention of these activities is included.)

- Omit a statement of recommendation.

- Refrain from qualifying a statement of recommendation. "I recommend Thomas to any district looking for a competent beginning teacher."

- Include a statement that indicates the mentor is willing to talk further about a specific concern. "If you would like more details about Thomas's work with diverse learners, please give me a call." (But be sure you are willing to speak candidly to the hiring personnel when they call.)

Sample Letters of Recommendation

Figures 8.7, 8.8, and 8.9 are some examples of letters written for beginning teachers both at the student-teaching and 1st-year levels. Although these do not propose to address all of the suggestions for effective letters

DIALOGUE

Dialogue: Letters of Recommendation

After reading the examples in Figures 8.7, 8.8, and 8.9, identify the components included that reflect suggestions on the previous pages. Then discuss the effect you think each letter might have on a potential employer with another mentor. If you are working alone, write down the effect you think these letters might have and reflect on their implications.

Figure 8.7 Sample Letter 1

To Whom It May Concern:

It is indeed a rare pleasure to write this letter of recommendation for _____, who is completing his first year of teaching seventh-grade science as my mentee at Central Middle School.

In nearly 40 years I have had the pleasure of working with many outstanding beginning teachers. None better than _____. Since he appeared in my doorway this fall, it's been a joy to watch him with students and to experience his competence and enthusiasm. _____ is always well prepared, and he is a powerful role model for students every day. His deeply personal approach demands their attention, and his wealth of relevant examples immerses the students in problems they care about.

His ability to communicate with students at both ends of the ability spectrum is uncommon. Whether he is helping an advanced section of earth science students or students at risk, his skills are remarkable. His students more than respect him. They love him! And they love what they are becoming because of his strong positive influence in their lives.

_____ is also an inspirational coach with all the maturity and perspective that such a position requires.

Having said all of this, you will be delighted to know that no matter how good it gets . . . _____ is ALWAYS looking to do it BETTER! I have never worked with anyone so willing to listen, to study, to research, to reflect, to invest so many of his resources and so much of his time to become a better teacher.

If you are fortunate enough to hire _____, your faculty and students will have a rendezvous with excellence!

Sincerely,

Figure 8.8   Sample Letter 2

To Whom It May Concern:

I have served this past year as a mentor to _____ during her first year teaching third grade at Village Elementary. _____ has focused her learning this year on classroom management and has come a long way. Students now know what to expect from _____'s classroom.

_____ has experimented with many instructional models and has become especially proficient at direct instruction. Students are on task and have many opportunities to work independently to hone their skills. _____ uses creative activities to get the students' attention and provides step-by-step guidance as students acquire new information.

Throughout this year, _____ has worked hard to facilitate her students' learning. Her willingness to take my suggestions and implement them into her lessons has been impressive. I know she has the potential to develop into a competent teacher.

If you would like to call me to discuss _____'s teaching skills, please do not hesitate. You may reach me at _____.

Sincerely,

Figure 8.9 Sample Letter 3

To Whom It May Concern:

The Algebra II classes conducted by _____ during her student teaching at Wilson High School clearly reflected her commitment to student-centered teaching and learning. As her college supervisor, I had the opportunity to observe _____ as she worked to hone her skills during this 14-week experience. _____'s strong knowledge base, her skill in planning lessons that engage students in their learning, and her ability to create an atmosphere in her classroom where math is relevant and fun identifies her as an outstanding beginning teacher.

_____'s knowledge of her subject area was apparent in her explanations to students in both Algebra II and her Functions, Statistics, and Trigonometry (FST) classes. When asked questions by students, she would not only provide answers that clarified the issue, but she also invited the students into the discussion of the problem with statements such as "Do you interpret that as . . .? Here's the way I see it . . . what do you think?" She placed students in work groups to share their understanding as they worked on problems that used information learned in class. _____'s ability to facilitate learning through her interaction with all the groups was the key to the success of this approach. In addition to the teaching of Algebra II and FST, _____ also tutored a struggling student in geometry, a demonstration of _____'s breadth of knowledge in mathematics.

_____'s lessons are carefully planned, and she uses her students' prior knowledge as a stepping stone upon which to build successive learning experiences. Her specific objectives go beyond the text to include the development of group interaction skills and the ability to problem-solve. To accomplish these objectives, _____ instituted a brain teaser of the day for students to work on as she began class and took attendance. These brain teasers stretched the students' thinking and provided an opportunity for them to apply mathematical logic to solve problems that often did not involve numbers.

_____ often asked students to describe their work, at the board or to their teammates, to facilitate their ability to communicate mathematically. Her careful attention to detail and use of a variety of resources, both print and technology, assist her in her teaching.

The greatest gift that _____ brings to her students is her willingness to create a classroom where math makes sense to students and where the joy of mathematics is celebrated. _____ often provided brief mathematical biographies to give a human face to the development of math concepts. The learning teams in her classes were all named for famous mathematicians, and _____ intentionally balanced the names of well-known male mathematicians with more current female individuals to provide role models for all of her students.

_____ worked to connect math concepts with the real world. Her students shot baskets one day to study the arc of the path of the ball into the basket. Students used their heights to physically create a bell curve and had to develop real life models to support statistical algorithms. Watching a group of students shout out, "I love FST!" when it had the correct answer to a problem on a unit review in _____'s class was a perfect example of a joyful learning experience.

All of this student-centered learning required _____ to be very clear and specific about her expectations for student behavior. _____ met this challenge by developing clear guidelines and rules for learning activities and by strengthening her communication style to provide a stronger presence in the classroom.

There are few beginning teachers who reflect as carefully on their teaching and work to compensate for lessons that need additional time or a different approach to support student learning than _____. The school district that adds _____ to its staff will not only be gaining a competent teacher of mathematics, but a teacher that focuses on engaging students in their learning. In addition, her ability to work effectively with her cooperating teacher and other colleagues identifies her as a strong asset to any school district. I highly recommend her!

Sincerely,

presented above, they are representative of letters that have been written with those criteria in mind.

Recommendation letters can be crafted to indicate areas the mentee has mastered as well as to identify red flags for areas that need future growth.

Although writing the letters is often the official culminating duty of a mentor as the mentoring relationship draws to a close, it is important that experienced educators continue to provide support for novice teachers in informal and casual settings. Ongoing support is the key to effective mentoring. Some programs continue across several years, some are only in place for the first year a teacher is in the classroom. Even when your mentoring relationship is no longer required, take the time to check in with your former mentee. A mentor who stops in and inquires how a former mentee is doing or how things are going is providing ongoing support. Regardless of the program time frame and structure, effective mentoring is all about relationships. So don't abandon your mentee at the end of the year. No matter how long they've been teaching, when teachers feel supported by colleagues, they become more effective teachers, and their students become better learners.

Resource A

Mentoring Projects

While mentors are reading and discussing the ideas in this book, they may find that they want to translate their thinking into action. In addition, some mentoring programs have the expectation that participants will apply their new knowledge in a way that provides additional materials and support for novice teachers. The following is a brief list of projects that can enhance individual mentoring skills as well as strengthen mentoring programs and interactions. The completion of these projects should result in a useful tool or resource for mentors and mentees to use during their work together.

PROJECT: NOVICE TEACHER RESOURCE BOOK ■

In a packet or notebook, mentors can gather together all of the relevant information that they believe a new teacher in their building should have. Mentors can go beyond the administrative documents to include helpful hints as well as insights into the traditions, processes, and procedures that are a part of the school culture. Because teacher handbooks can contain an overwhelming amount of information, it might be helpful for mentors to provide a quick tips or an FAQ (frequently asked questions) format to help new teachers wade through this information to find what they need. The development of a Web page for new teachers that also could be available for parents or other community members might be another helpful format for sharing this information.

Suggestions for content:

All or some of the following ideas could be included in a mentor's packet or on the mentoring Web page:

- All pertinent information (handbook information) about the school/district (e.g., forms, discipline policy and procedures)
- A letter of welcome to the mentee from the mentor outlining the mentoring program and his or her expectations for the experience

- The mentor's plan for developing a relationship with his or her mentee (e.g., having lunch, meeting for coffee)
- A plan or timeline for introducing mentees to the facilities and to faculty and administration
- A schedule for creating a system of peer support for mentees (explaining how mentors plan to get them together with other student teachers or 1st-year teachers)
- Times for conferences, meetings, and observations (to allow for a gradual induction for student teachers, for trust-building for both 1st-year and student teachers) or a plan to set up convenient meeting times
- A list of the mentor's prep times, extracurricular duties, and responsibilities (as well as dates of conferences, team meetings, curriculum committee meetings, athletic meets, and so on, that could or should be attended)
- A format or schedule for videotaping one of the mentee's lessons
- A suggested format for lesson plans that reflect the lens that will be used during observations, if the lens is predetermined by the school or district
- State and/or district curricula, scope and sequence, units, and/or other grade level course expectations
- Model lesson plan ideas for the mentee to try
- Ideas and opportunities for team teaching
- For student teachers, a format that will accommodate all the college's requests (forms, due dates, evaluations)
- A process for 1st-year teachers to address the expectations of the program (scheduled workshops, meetings, and so on)
- Ideas for facilitating good communication during the mentoring experience

■ PROJECT: FORMATIVE ACTION PLAN

Using the action plan provided in Chapter 4 as a formative tool, mentors can develop a plan to enhance their own knowledge in an area that will increase their ability to support a novice teacher. Mentors can share their completed action plans with buddy mentors to reflect on how the plan is progressing. Some ideas for the plan are as follows:

- Gathering information on best practices in the mentor's content area
- Practicing communication skills with another mentor
- Reading articles or a book on mentoring
- Setting up a schedule for mini-conversations at lunch or prep time with another mentor to talk through issues—and following through on these conversations

■ PROJECT: SHARING YOUR EXPERTISE

Mentors can create a plan for sharing their expertise with other potential mentor-teachers in their schools: presenting at inservice programs, duplicating project ideas, or coordinating cooperating teacher or student gatherings. Mentors should present their plan to the administration or staff development office for consideration.

PROJECT: REFLECTIONS ■

Mentors can keep journals of their thoughts as they work through this text or as they develop their mentoring skills. They can continue writing in their journal as they work with their mentees and can use their journal as a springboard for conversations with their mentees, for ideas for action research, or for sharing stories and experiences. Mentors should include any insights, personal growth, or added awareness that they develop. They should specifically identify how they plan to use their journals in their work with mentees.

PROJECT: E-MENTORING AND ■ ELECTRONIC DISCUSSIONS

Setting up an e-mail address that can be used to pose questions or as a Listserv where novice teachers can ask questions of any or all mentors can provide quick answers to a new teacher's concerns. A mentor or the director of the mentoring program should be identified to manage the conversation. Questions about content or grade level might be forwarded to teachers who are not on the Listserv, and answers sent to all novice teachers. Providing novice teachers with a network of resources can extend support beyond a single mentor and create an environment where the entire school embraces the concept of helping new teachers. Some mentor programs expect mentees to log on and read and submit comments and questions as a part of facilitating the interaction, but a volunteer program can be more inviting to the novice teacher. In either format, extending the support network in order to provide quick response is the key, because if no one responds to the questions posed, the new teachers will not be encouraged to participate.

Resource B

Role-Plays

Mentors can extend their learning—especially in the area of communication—by practicing their verbal skills. The following scenarios provide problematic situations that mentors might experience. Mentors can role-play these situations with another mentor and try to think on their feet. If possible, mentor pairs should have a third mentor serve as observer to note their responses. Those taking part can debrief the role-play and consider additional responses that would create a positive ending to the scenario.

Participants in the role-play should determine whether the mentor and mentee in each situation are getting together for an informal meeting or a conference following an observation. The scenario description serves as a mental script, directing how each individual should start and focus his or her thoughts in this conversation. Some situations reveal the inner thoughts of the participants, some give outside information or describe events that have occurred. Those who are role-playing the mentee should try to be as realistic as possible. Their dialogue should be typical for a beginner in each situation. Mentors should implement effective communication and problem-solving skills and try to work toward a resolution of the problem. In addition, role-play groups should include in their debriefings a discussion of what might have created the situations and what mentors can do proactively to prevent this problem from happening.

SCENARIOS ■

Scenario 1

Role A: You are a mentor. You met and briefly observed a mentee two weeks ago. There were indications that the mentee has some difficulty with appropriate use of the English language—you heard frequent use of inappropriate grammar, and she seemed to lack clarity regarding expectations for students.

Role B: You are a new teacher (a mentee). You have been teaching for three weeks. Things seem to be going well except for the difficulty of knowing how much to plan. Part of what you are concerned about is knowing or anticipating how long activities will last. You do not remember the mentor's first name.

Scenario 2

Role A: You are a new teacher (a mentee). You are having some significant discipline problems in your classes. It seems like weeks since the mentor has offered assistance. This upsets you.

Role B: You are a new mentor. You have not checked in on your new mentee as much as others have because she seems to want independence and she seemed competent in previous discussions. You must be at an inservice that you are facilitating in 40 minutes. The drive is minimally 30 minutes. You also really need to use the restroom.

Scenario 3

Role A: You are a mentor. You are waiting for a mentee's prep period to begin. You are reviewing notes concerning the progress of the mentee toward goals that he set for trying some new assessment techniques.

Role B: You are a veteran teacher. You have noticed that the mentee who teaches next door to you has deviated from the testing procedures to which you and another colleague have become accustomed. Also, there seems to be a lot of noise in the mentee's room during project time (whatever that is). You feel you must tell this new teacher's mentor about these troublesome activities for the good of the students. You approach the mentor in the faculty room and immediately start in with your concerns.

Scenario 4

Role A: You are a new teacher (a mentee). You are experiencing some personal problems (finances, car troubles, loneliness) that are making it difficult to be happy in your new job and new community. You have not shared this with others but hope to seek the advice of your mentor.

Role B: You are a mentor. You observed your mentee last week. Prior to the observation it was decided that you would watch the questioning techniques of your mentee. In the observation you noted the following:

- The mentee called on the boys much more frequently than the girls, despite a 50-50 split in gender distribution.
- The mentee tended to identify the student who would answer the question prior to asking it.
- Five seconds or longer was given to students on the higher level questions—much more than was given on the factual ones.

SOURCE: The four scenarios were developed by Mike Miller, dean of education at Mankato State University, Mankato, Minnesota, and Marc Boehlke, formerly of the Minnesota Department of Children, Families, and Learning. Used with permission.

ADDITIONAL MENTOR/MENTEE SITUATIONS ■

Directions: These situations do not provide specifics for mentors or mentees and can be used in two ways. Mentors can consider and discuss what they would do in each of them beforehand. Participants should role-play the situations, articulating a specific response as if they were communicating directly with the mentee. Mentee responses should also be role-played.

Situation 1

First-year teacher Mary is overwhelmed by the paperwork required for special education. She has a caseload of 30 students in the grade school she works in. She comes to you, her mentor, and says, "I am struggling to keep up with all of the students' paperwork. I just don't know what to do. What is the most important thing to focus on? I want to connect with these kids on a more personal level, but it seems I am always working on IEPs! What should I do?"

Situation 2

"So I know I am supposed to be keeping this kid on track and supporting his learning but I really don't like him. He is so mean and negative all the time . . . nothing is his fault, everyone is out to get him, and all of us teachers are stupid. I just don't know what to do. His diagnosis of EBD explains his behavior, but I just think he's a bully. How can I get past this so I can stand to work with him?" What do you say when your mentee shares this with you?

Situation 3

Roger, a mentor, is stopped in the hall by his mentee, Laura. Laura says, "I have such an energetic group of third graders. I really like to get them actively involved in their learning, but yesterday the math manipulatives were getting tossed around the classroom. I told them we wouldn't be using them for a while because of that. Now I am feeling like I have punished the kids who really need to use manipulatives by going back to paper-and-pencil work, and the other third-grade teacher isn't too happy with me about this. I don't want to seem like a pushover, so I am not sure I want to go back on what I said about no manipulatives. But I am not sure if I made the right decision—what do you think?"

Situation 4

Your mentee, Kristen, sent home a volunteer sign-up sheet requesting parents to come in and help with reading support and other interactive classroom supports for her first graders. The request form encouraged "all parents, guardians, or grandparents to come join in on the learning." One family replied that both parents would be able to volunteer in the classroom, and the signatures indicated that the parents were a gay couple. Another parent-reply specifically indicated that they knew that a student had gay parents and requested that this couple not be involved in the classroom with their child. Kristen hoped to create a learning community with the families of her students through parental interaction. "I don't know what to do about this situation," she says to you. "What should I do?" How will you respond to Kristen?

Situation 5

"Okay, I know I am a beginner," Leo states, "but as the special education teacher, I have some valid suggestions for the classroom teachers I am working with this year. But whenever I offer to sit down and work with them to provide support for the mainstreamed students, some of these people really seem to brush me off. They are always too busy to sit down and talk, or they just say, 'Okay, whatever you want to do,' when I make a suggestion. I need to figure out a way to connect with them. I am really interested in working together in the classroom—doing more of a team approach. I just don't know how to get to a level where these more experienced teachers will listen to me. Can you help me with this?"

Situation 6

Nick, a ninth-grade, 1st-year English teacher, comes to you, his mentor, with the following complaint: "My kids just don't read the assigned literature at night. I can't hold a discussion or go over any of the literary components of a work when they haven't read the assignment. So I am giving a quiz each day. Lots of the kids aren't doing very well. I really don't like the quiz mentality, but I am not sure I should give them time to read in class. I think some of them might fail because of these quizzes. What do you do when kids don't do the homework assigned? How can I get them to do the reading each night?"

Situation 7

Josephina, a high school art teacher who is in her first year of teaching, stops you, her mentor, in the cafeteria. "I am trying to get these kids excited about art," she says. "I have them drawing art for a cover of a CD by their favorite group. The problems I have are tardies, absences, and kids who just take forever to get started working. It seems like I am always busy keeping track of who is here or late, and so some of the students just kick back and don't get started until I get on their case. I would think they would enjoy doing this project, but some of them have to be prodded to get out their supplies and get started. Is there anything I should be doing to get them going more quickly? I mean, they do get working eventually, and their products are looking pretty good, but it seems like we waste so much time!"

Situation 8

Your mentee, Jerome, a 1st-year math teacher, comes in to see you after school. "I am really having problems with my Connections class. We are progressing through the book pretty quickly. I have used some group-learning activities, and we have worked problems at the board every day, and I told them that they need to know this stuff for the upcoming test. These are kids who hate math, but they need to be able to pass the state test. I am trying to make this more hands-on—and the book has some great investigations, but it just isn't working. I don't get what their problem is. I get comments like 'This stuff is stupid' and 'Why do we need to know this anyway?' I told them that they need this to graduate but I still hear these complaints. I am getting so frustrated!"

Situation 9

"If one more kid tells me that what we are learning is boring, I will scream!" Maranda said. A 1st-year teacher, she has come into her mentor's office to talk. "I really work to get them to read primary documents in our history class. We read the U.S. Constitution the other day. I try to connect this to their lives, to the fact that they will be voting members of society pretty soon. But I keep hearing these mumbled comments: 'This is sooo boring!' After all the work I put into making lesson plans—it makes me pretty upset."

Situation 10

Alisha, an African American, 1st-year, social studies teacher, has really gotten her ninth-grade civics classes excited about their study of civil rights. She is planning to organize a student rally to point out the issues of racism that are still occurring in the school and in other institutions. She comes to you for advice on how to get such a rally started. "I want my students to learn how to be advocates for their own rights," she tells you. You know that about 60% of her classes are composed of Black students, the other 40% is a mix of Caucasian, Asian, and Latino students. The community has not been very active regarding issues of diversity, and race issues are rarely discussed openly. What are your reactions to Alisha's proposal? What suggestions will you give to Alisha?

Resource C

How to Use This Text: A Guide for Individuals and Facilitators

This book is designed to enhance the skills of educators who assume the role of mentor by providing, through dialogue with their peers, a means of reflecting on the process of guiding novice teachers. It is most helpful if teachers using this book have a partner or a group of colleagues with whom to have such a dialogue because the process of sharing experiences and discussing ideas for helping new teachers contributes to the development of strong mentoring skills. Mentors who are working alone can read through the text and consider the issues presented in the dialogue sections, write down answers to questions, and come back later to reflect on their ideas. Discussions via individual or group e-mail can also provide a means for sharing views and responding to the text. However, the dialogue sections are most effective when conducted in person with other experienced teachers who will also serve as mentors.

Learning from the work of other educators, sharing stories and ideas, and discussing and thinking about experiences and suggestions will have a more profound effect on a mentor's development than reading this text alone. A veteran teacher's ideas and knowledge can reaffirm another's skills or lead others to explore new avenues in their teaching and thinking. This book provides opportunities for veteran educators to discuss, debate, share, explore, and learn together in order to best facilitate the development of novice teachers. Thus, the village elders of the educational community can extend their knowledge in order to pass along their expertise and skills.

Before beginning the dialogues in this text, mentors may choose to take the pre-program questionnaire presented in Figure 8.5. It provides mentors with a snapshot of their knowledge as they begin reading this book. Mentors can use the results of the questionnaire to individualize the mentoring process to best meet their needs. After mentors have completed the book, the follow-up questionnaire in Figure 8.6 can be used to identify growth. These questionnaires provide mentors with before-and-after pictures of what they have learned about the mentoring process and can be helpful as a program evaluation tool.

Some of the opportunities for dialogue in the text are geared specifically toward the development of mentoring skills and should be considered by all future mentors. Some dialogue topics are suggestions for future conversation between the mentor and mentee to enhance their relationship. Because mentors are the experienced members of the relationship, the majority of the dialogues are focused on using and strengthening the mentor's knowledge and skills so they can take the lead in interactions. All the tools, charts, role-plays, questions, and scenarios are meant to foster a positive mentoring relationship. As identified by Rippon & Martin (2002), role-play, simulation, and interactive sessions focused on the role and responses required of mentors are effective tools in developing necessary feedback and communication skills. Exercises may be modified to fit different situations, but the goal is to avoid the random conversations which can occur in interactions between teachers and their protégés when little thought is given to structuring these conversations. Focusing discussions, acting out scenarios, and role-playing using the text suggestions will help maximize the potential of mentor-mentee conversations. With that in mind, mentors should consider this book as a part of their ongoing learning process. Think about the ideas and situations presented during your preparation as a mentor and return to the text for suggestions and support when addressing new issues with your mentee.

If the text is used as a resource in a more formal study group or workshop setting, a group leader or trainer may choose to structure participant interactions in a variety of ways. The text itself provides a step-by-step process. Participants can begin by reading the text to inform themselves about mentoring concepts, then follow up by engaging in the dialogues and reflections that provide practice in the skill area. Facilitators can organize workshop sessions by using each chapter of the text sequentially to provide a structure for meetings. Reading assignments can be given prior to group sessions, and the meeting time can be spent in dialogues, activities, and reflections. Sessions can focus on parts of each chapter or one entire chapter during shorter meetings, or facilitators may choose to combine chapters into a longer workshop format over a full day or two. The guide that follows is designed to assist mentor trainers as they use the text and shape workshop experiences for future mentors. Whether working alone or with others, the structure of this text will provide the reader with opportunities to gain knowledge and practice skills that will enhance his or her ability to effectively mentor novice teachers.

FACILITATOR'S GUIDE TO ■
SETTING UP A WORKSHOP

Workshop Objective/Goal

Upon completion of this workshop, participants will be able to answer the critical questions and use their newly acquired knowledge and skills to effectively mentor a novice teacher.

The goal of this workshop is to involve everyone in actual conversation in order to practice the mentoring skills identified, so it is important that people feel comfortable with each other. Use name tags, provide refreshments, and set aside time for introductions. Arrange the room to allow for ease of movement and to encourage interaction.

Workshop Outline

The workshop is based on the 16 critical questions for guiding the dialogue process listed on page 135. All of them may be used, or the facilitator or participants may determine the most pressing questions to address during the training. Questions to be addressed in each session can be posted on the board at the beginning of the day.

Workshop Process

Opportunities for dialogue, discussion, and role-plays are provided within each chapter. In addition, this workshop guide includes facilitator comments, assigned readings, and additional activities. As you walk your participants through the text, use the questions to start a new topic, the readings to provide background information, and then engage participants in the interactive conversations and activities.

Reading Assignments

To break up reading assignments when workshop sessions are spread across several days, give the reading assignments as homework. This will shorten your time in the workshop session and allow participants to focus on the dialogues and exchange of ideas during their time together. Participants can read several sections or all of a chapter and come prepared for the dialogue and activities.

Facilitator's Role

All participants need to feel comfortable with processes and interactions. The session leader should be actively engaged, ready to step in and model any dialogue process or conversation and able to take part in any role-play. The facilitator's role is to encourage but not overwhelm participants.

In addition, the facilitator needs to manage the time and interactions within the workshop. This involves providing structure for each activity; helping the group transition from readings to the active learning required to practice and develop skills. Organizing the space of the workshop to maximize comfort and ease of conversation is also important, as is setting a time frame for each component of the session to ensure that all concepts are addressed. Facilitators may want to provide different formats for interaction, pairing individuals, moving people into small groups, and providing space for role-plays. Input from participants should be gathered and recorded on overheads or chart paper for future reference. Facilitators need to observe, monitor and adjust the time spent on readings, dialogues, and activities to ensure that participants meet all the objectives of the workshop.

Critical Questions for Guiding the Dialogue Process

These questions can be restated as objectives and all (or some) of the questions/objectives can become the focus for your workshop(s).

1. What is a mentor? Why is one needed in education?

2. Why be a mentor teacher?

3. How do I share my vision of teaching? How can metaphors help with this process?

4. What are my expectations for the mentoring experience?

5. What are the roles of the mentor, mentee, administrative supervisor (or college supervisor)?

6. How do I build trust?

7. How do I get off to a good start with my mentee?

8. How does communication impact the mentoring relationship?

9. How do I effectively interact with mentees who may have differing perspectives and backgrounds?

10. What are my mentee's needs?

11. How do I support my mentee and meet his or her needs?

12. How do I give suggestions, help, and advice to meet my mentee's needs?

13. Are there models that can help the mentoring and observation process?

14. What do I need to know about conferencing skills?

15. What are some data-gathering techniques I can use?

16. Evaluation—what is its role in mentoring programs?

■ WORKSHOP SESSIONS

Introductory Session

Opening Comments: Introduce yourself and take a moment to welcome your participants. Mention your own teaching background and then ask for individuals to introduce themselves. Request that each participant tell the group his or her teaching assignment and the reason for attending this workshop.

Purpose of Workshop: After the introductions, comment on the reasons people are attending this workshop. Display an overhead of the 16 critical questions for guiding the dialogue process noted above. Explain that upon completion of this workshop, participants will be able to answer the critical questions and use their newly acquired knowledge and skills to effectively mentor novice teachers. Ask if anyone has questions about the direction this course will take.

Pre-Workshop Questionnaire: To identify prior knowledge, have participants complete the questionnaire in Figure 8.5. At the end of the workshop, participants will complete a similar questionnaire, and the results of both can be compared to determine the impact of the workshop.

Question 1: What is a mentor and why is one needed in education? (25 minutes)

Opener: Ask all participants to think back to their first year of teaching and to think about the best moment of that experience. What happened? How did this positive experience come about?

Partner Sharing (10 minutes): Ask participants to share their best experience with someone sitting near them.

Now ask participants to think about the worst experience they had that first year. What was that event? What caused it? What could have helped avoid this difficulty?

Have participants share this experience with the same person they just spoke with.

Facilitator's note: If you see someone who is not talking to anyone or who is without a conversation partner, be sure to connect them to a group or talk with that individual yourself. Do not let anyone sit quietly. Provide them with an opportunity to talk about their experiences.

Group Debrief (10 minutes): Ask the following questions and briefly respond to comments that are given:

- Will someone please share, if they feel comfortable, what they heard during these brief conversations?
- What emotions surfaced when you revisited these experiences?
- Did anyone have someone to whom they turned during this first year? If so, how did that occur? Was it helpful?

Summarize (5 minutes): Identify the need for mentors (use the Preface of this text to provide specific rationale and references).

Question 2: Why be a mentor teacher? (20 minutes)

Reading Assignment (5 minutes): Chapter 1, pages 1 to 4, What Is a Mentor? Why We Need Mentors, Why We Need Mentor Training, and Why Be a Mentor?

Group Discussion (15 minutes): Invite comments or reactions to the reading assignment.

Ask participants to share their reasons for serving as a mentor.

Question 3: How do you share your vision of teaching? How can metaphors help? (60 to 70 minutes)

Reading Assignment (10 minutes): Chapter 1, pages 4–7, A Personal Vision of Teaching

Individual Activity (10 minutes): Ask participants to brainstorm a metaphor (or simile) that reflects their own visions of teaching. (Pass out note cards for participants to jot down their metaphor.)

Partner Sharing (15 minutes): After participants have written down their metaphors, ask them to look at page 5, Figure 1.1. Ask participants to find another partner and complete the process of discussing and refining personal metaphors for teaching. Point out that sometimes our metaphors are not clear to others, so this is an opportunity to clarify.

Explain that each person needs to explain his metaphor, and then his partner needs to verbalize his understanding of that metaphor. This process will help each mentor come away with a clear image of his individual vision of teaching, which he can now share with his future mentee.

Be sure to point out that this activity is an example of the process of listening and clarifying, which will be an important part of any mentoring conversation.

Group Activity (10 minutes): Ask participants to share their metaphors and ask if their partners clearly understood their vision the first time or if they had to refine their metaphors a bit.

Point out the metaphor chart on page 6 (Figure 1.2) and put it on the overhead. Identify for participants that this chart is a means for them to use their metaphor with their mentee to explain their personal vision of teaching. The chart also enables them to get a picture of their mentee's vision of teaching. The mentor already has completed the first step in this chart, but the process of completing it with a mentee will enable the two of them to begin to talk about their visions of teaching so that they gain some insights into each other's point of view.

Dialogue (15 minutes): Remembering Experiences, Chapter 1, page 9

Ask participants to read through the questions under the heading, To Start the Conversation. (Put these questions on an overhead projector.) Explain that the participants will now be participating in a dialogue with a partner about their earlier experiences. The questions will guide the conversations. Point out that there will be a series of guiding questions for reflecting about their dialogues; extend the conversation using the questions at the bottom of page 9.

Ask the participants to read the questions through and then to share their thoughts with a partner. After participants have discussed the questions, ask for feedback from the group.

Group Debrief (10 minutes): Display the following questions on the overhead projector. Ask the questions and briefly respond to participants' answers.

Do you remember how you handled the problematic event?

Do you think you might have responded differently if you had been able to talk about your ideas and plans with another teacher?

Did anyone offer you advice that you felt was not helpful?

Did your principal or another administrator provide you with help?

If an administrator did provide help, how did this feel to you as a beginner?

Questions 4 and 5: What are your expectations for the mentoring experience? What are the roles of the mentor, mentee, and administrative supervisor? (50 minutes)

Reading Assignment (15 minutes): Chapter 1, pages 8–13, Role Descriptions

Ask for comments and reflections from participants about the reading.

Dialogue (15 minutes): Mentoring Roles, Chapter 1, pages 13–17

Have participants read the dialogue directions on page 13 and then complete the expectations for mentor-teachers on pages 15 and 16.

Point out that it is helpful for ALL members of the triad to complete ALL of the expectations checklists and then to discuss them. These checklists can then serve as a starting point for developing clear expectations for all participants in a mentoring program.

For the purposes of this workshop, you might assign groups of participants to complete each expectation list from the perspective of the mentee and supervisor and then share them. This will help provide some perspective from the point of view of the mentee and supervisor, even if they are not present at the workshop. In this way, you can give participants an opportunity to discuss all of the roles and their potential impact on each other. Administrators in attendance should complete the checklist for supervisors. If possible, share examples of checklists previously completed by 1st-year mentees prior to this session.

Partner Sharing (10 minutes): After participants have completed the checklists, have them turn to a partner and discuss what they agree on and what they see differently about the roles of mentor. (Or discuss the roles of mentee and supervisor, if you have anyone completing those checklists.)

Group Debrief (10 minutes): Use the following questions to invite feedback about the process.

What were the differences between your view of the role of the mentor (or mentee or supervisor)?

How might these differences create conflict or misconceptions during the mentoring process?

How might you address these differences if you and your mentee view the role of mentor differently?

How might the use of these checklists serve to clarify expectations for all members of your mentor program, and how can you incorporate them into your work with mentees and supervisors?

Questions 6 and 7: How do you build trust? How do you get off to a good start with your mentee? (20–30 minutes)

Opener: Explain that we talk a lot about building trust in a relationship and that our good friends are usually people we trust. Then explain that mentees need to trust their mentor before they will share their true feelings and concerns. Ask, "How do you develop trust when you are entering a new relationship?" Restate responses so all can hear.

Reading Assignment (10 minutes): Chapter 2, pages 19–21, Building Trust

Scenario (20 minutes): Trust Building, Chapter 2, page 22

Ask for volunteers to read the two parts of the trust-building scene on page 22. Then ask participants to identify the efforts the mentor was making to build trust, using the debriefing questions at the bottom of the page. You can extend this conversation by reading the suggestions on page 22, then asking the participants what other ideas they have for creating a conversation that provides for self-disclosure and begins to build trust. Ask for feedback following this activity.

Question 8: How does communication impact the mentoring relationship? (90 minutes)

Opener: Ask your participants to think about this: "The choice of words in conversation and the tone of voice used can have a major impact on the message being heard. When developing a supportive relationship, it is important that the mentor remain aware of the impact of their conversation."

Reading Assignment (10 minutes): Chapter 2, pages 21 and 23–24, Open Communication

Group Activity (10 minutes): Review Figure 2.1. Discuss the value of setting ground rules early in the relationship. Ask participants for some suggestions for ground rules that they might generate. Consider some ground rules that may provide a sense of comfort for the mentee.

Use an overhead projector, white board, or chart paper to record the suggested ground rules and discuss participants' reaction to beginning a relationship with something as formal as ground rules.

Read aloud (or ask a participant to read aloud) the section on verbal messages on pages 24–26. Ask: "Do we always know what people really mean when they communicate?" Ask participants to share their own examples of being misunderstood due to a choice of words.

Scenario (20 minutes): Focus On a Verbal Message, Chapter 2, page 25

Ask for two volunteers to read the scenario on page 25, then ask participants to turn to a partner and debrief using the suggestions following the scene. Then read the bottom of page 25 and top of page 26 for other mentors' ideas.

Ask participants to read pages 26–27 to expand their understanding of the importance of checking signals.

Dialogue (10 minutes): Exact Language, Chapter 2, page 27

Have participants select partners and follow the directions to complete the exercise.

When finished, ask participants if they found that they had similar interpretations of the word choices and to consider what the difference in word choice might make in their conversations.

Discussion (10 minutes): Chapter 2, pages 28–29, Nonverbal Messages

Have participants read the selection. Then ask if they have any examples of situations in which their tone of voice or body language didn't fit what they said, and consequently if there was miscommunication. (Share an example of your own.)

Dialogue (10 minutes): Nonverbal Practices 1 & 2, Chapter 2, pages 29 and 30

Ask participants to work with partners to complete the exercises and discuss the follow-up questions.

Question 9: How do I effectively interact with mentees who may have differing perspectives and backgrounds? (20–30 minutes)

Reading Assignment (10 minutes): Chapter 2, pages 30–31

Discussion (20 minutes): Ask participants for examples of situations where proximity or turn-taking might have been an aspect of the communication. Remind them that these cultural generalizations are simply that—generalizations—and that they need to learn more about their mentee's culture to ensure that they can communicate in a way that supports each other's cultural perspective.

Read pages 31–33 and review Figure 2.2. Ask mentors to share how they feel about working with experienced colleagues.

Question 10: What are my mentee's needs? (15–25 minutes)

Opener: Explain that just as students in our classrooms come to us with a variety of learning styles and levels of preparation, so too do beginning teachers. Ask: "So if your mentee has difficulties meeting the expectations for a beginning teacher, how can you support his or her ongoing learning?" Put answers and ideas on the board.

Reading Assignment (10 minutes): Chapter 2, pages 35–38

Presentation (15 minutes): Display an overhead transparency of page 38. When presenting this overhead, point out that beginning teachers need support to expand their vision of their classroom.

Question 11: How do I support my mentee and meet his or her needs? (90 minutes)

(Note to facilitator: This session is divided into three parts.)

Opener: Explain that during this session, participants will be discussing ways mentors can support their mentees and meet their needs. Display and read aloud the bulleted list of needs on page 38 on an overhead transparency or the board. Refer to this list as you progress through this session.

Part 1: The Need for Empathy and Personal Support (30–40 minutes total)
Explain that the emotional needs of new teachers can be surprising to mentors if they don't stop and recall the pressures they faced during their first year of teaching.

Reading Assignment (10 minutes): Chapter 3, pages 38–40, The Need for Empathy and Personal Support
After reading, ask for participants to share any experiences they might have had that were challenging emotionally during the beginning of their careers.

Scenario (20 minutes): Providing Emotional Support, Chapter 3, page 41
Ask for two volunteers to read the scene.

Dialogue (10 minutes): Emotional Support, Chapter 3, page 42
Following the scenario, have participants select partners and practice sharing feedback with one another as if they were speaking to their mentees, using support statements from Figure 3.2.

Part 2: The Need to Accurately See What Is Happening in the Classroom (30–50 minutes total)
Explain that now participants will develop skills in observing and conferencing with mentees so they can provide a mirror into their classrooms and meet that basic need.

Reading Assignment (10 minutes): Chapter 3, pages 40 and 42–44, The Need to Accurately See What Is Happening in the Classroom
Have participants read this overview of the need to offer mentees a mirror of their classrooms.

Scenario (20 minutes): Mirroring a Classroom, Chapter 3, page 43
Explain that gathering nonjudgmental data from an observation is challenging. Tell participants that they will practice making notes of an observation using the form on page 45, Figure 3.3.
Ask three volunteers to read/enact the scene on page 43. Have participants turn to the form on page 45 to jot down their thoughts, during or immediately after the scene is read.

Resource Figure 1   Three-Column Observation Form

Tell participants that as they watch and listen to the role-play, they should jot down on the form specific evidence describing what they see and hear and write personal thoughts or observations in the *I thought* column. This form is presented later in the data-gathering chapter, but introducing it here can be a helpful option for mentors as they work to find a comfortable means of documenting nonjudgmental comments.

I saw . . .	I heard . . .	I thought . . .
Guiding questions to probe what you saw or heard . . .		

Dialogue (10 minutes): Observation, Chapter 3, page 44

After observing the role-play, have partners share with one another what they saw and heard. Encourage them to use care in their tone and choice of words. Use the data you collected using Figure 3.3.

Ask participants if they have other thoughts or comments to make regarding the feedback from the observation. After the dialogue, ask how easy it was to gather data. Introduce Resource Figure 1 and redo the scenario from page 43. Have participants use Resource Figure 1, then discuss which form they prefer for gathering observational evidence. Use the copy above as an overhead to give an example, or make copies of this page for all participants.

Part 3: The Need for Guiding Questions (40–60 minutes total)

Explain that now participants will develop skills in observing and conferencing with mentees so they can provide a mirror into their classrooms and meet that basic need.

Reading Assignment (10 minutes): Chapter 3, pages 44, 46, The Need for Guiding Questions

Have participants read this section to develop an understanding of the use of guiding questions.

Scenario (20 minutes): Observation and Guiding Questions, Chapter 3, page 47

Have two volunteers read the scenario while participants observe and record notes using one of the observation forms described previously.

Following the role-play, have participants pretend that they are planning to use the form and the data they gathered from this brief observation to talk with the beginning teacher from the role-play. Encourage them to consider the types of questions they might ask and to write down any questions that they would ask this beginning teacher.

Dialogue (10 minutes): Reflecting on Guiding Questions, Chapter 3, page 47

Have participants share with a partner the questions they developed and would ask of the beginning teacher following the observation.

Next, have participants silently read "Scenario: Feedback Conversation" on page 48.

Dialogue (10 minutes): Guiding Questions, Chapter 3, page 49

Invite participants to reflect on "Scenario: Feedback Conversation" and discuss with a partner whether the questions they developed were similar to those in the dialogue.

Reading Assignment (10 minutes): Chapter 3, pages 49–51

Have participants read this section to review other options for guiding questions. Then ask participants what additional guiding questions among those suggested they might use.

Optional Practice Activity A (20 minutes): Explain that this activity will provide practice in asking guiding questions to shape a novice teacher's awareness of a problem.

Draw two columns on the board or on chart paper. Ask for participants to describe particular situations novice teachers face in the first column, and then have the group suggest guiding questions that might be used in that situation. If participants need a starting point, review the suggested guiding questions on pages 49–50. Ask volunteers to identify the questions that they might use or adapt for their future conversations related to the issues. List on the board the questions suggested by participants.

Optional Practice Activity B (20 minutes): Have participants engage in the role-play suggested on page 51.

Question 12: How do I give suggestions, help, and advice? What if my mentee struggles? (40–60 minutes)

Opener: Explain to participants that the way they provide support has much to do with a novice teacher's willingness and ability to follow up on their suggestions. When using evidence gathered during an observational process, it is important for mentors to stick to the facts so that the mentee can see and hear his or her classroom interactions. It can also be helpful to be more specific. Creating an action plan, or long-range plans, can help mentees structure their learning so that they focus on the areas of development that are most important. Providing resources for novice teachers is critical, as they will need specific information and suggestions in order to address the concerns identified in the action or the long-range plan.

Reading Assignment (10 minutes): Chapter 4, pages 53–55 (stopping before Steps 1–3)

Have participants read this section to review a process and a tool for giving advice and suggestions that provides specific support and direction for mentees. Encourage participants to review the sample action plan in Figure 4.1 on page 56 and notice its components.

Dialogue (10 minutes): Action Plan, Chapter 4, page 55

Invite participants to review the situation with a partner and generate an action plan using the format shown in Figure 4.2. Partners should outline the steps they think should be followed by this novice teacher to deal with the situation.

Next, have participants read the remainder of page 55 and page 57 to see some possible steps that might be implemented in an action plan for the situation described in the dialogue.

Discussion (20 minutes): To extend the conversation about action plans, ask the group the following questions:

Did your action plans have steps similar to those described in the text? What was different?

Why did you include these steps in your plan?

When do you think you will use action plans?

Should there be an expectation for novice teachers—that all beginners identify areas where they can grow and articulate their goals in an action plan? Why or why not?

Explain to participants that sometimes novice teachers face issues that are challenging, and some of these may cause the new teacher to struggle. Being honest with mentees can be the most helpful response in these situations.

Reading Assignment (10 minutes): Chapter 4, pages 58–63, The Need for Honesty

The need for honesty is described in this section. You may wish to have participants read this as homework or over lunch or a break, so they return ready to discuss these ideas. Have partners share their thoughts about action plans and long-range plans.

Dialogue (10 minutes): Working Through an Impasse, Chapter 4, page 63

For this dialogue, randomly assign each of the three bulleted situations to different small groups. Review the directions after the bullet points and ask participants to discuss how they would communicate their concerns to a novice teacher regarding the situation described. Ask for groups to share their thinking and then ask each group to focus on the questions for further thinking. Debrief with the entire group and write on the board, overhead, or chart paper the questions and participants' comments regarding each. Write an action plan as a group for one of the mentees from the dialogue.

Homework Assignment: Have participants read Chapter 4, pages 63–64, What Student Teachers Need, as homework.

When the participants regroup, ask if there are any comments regarding how mentors should deal with student teachers.

Question 13: Are there models that can help the mentoring process? (40 minutes)

Opener: Mention that all new teachers know that they will be evaluated by a supervisor at some point. It is important for the mentor to observe the mentee using the same lens that the administration will use during an evaluative observation. The coordination of this is vital. The mentor can use the lens as a talking point or a means of gathering evidence during an observation. A school or a district must be clear about its expectations for beginning teachers, and this articulation of expectations, in whatever form, must be the basis for their development. Without this coordination, a mentee may be caught off guard when a supervisor asks about different criteria or evaluates using a different tool because that may not have been the focus of the mentoring. While the mentor is not evaluating, using the evaluation instrument as a lens to observe a mentee ensures that the mentor, mentee, and supervisor are all working toward the same goals.

(Note: Facilitators can choose from one of three options for having participants examine the lenses used to observe and evaluate the mentee.)

Option 1

Reading Assignment (20 minutes): Chapter 5, pages 65–75, The Mentor's Lens

Have participants read and consider the various lenses used to observe and evaluate the mentee.

Activity (20 minutes): Chapter 5, page 76, Figure 5.15, Analysis of the Lenses

After participants have read about the lenses, have them use the form on page 76 to analyze them and determine which one they (or their district) would find most useful. Ask participants to share their perspectives with a partner.

Option 2

Reading Assignment (20 minutes): Selections from Chapter 5, pages 65–75

Rather than have individuals read all of the descriptions, divide the participants into four groups and assign one of the lenses (PATHWISE, Danielson's framework, INTASC, and *Dimensions of Learning*) to each group to read. Have each group summarize on chart paper or an overhead the key points of the lens.

Activity (20 minutes): Have each group report on the key points of the lens. After each group has shared its summary, use the form on page 76 to compare the lenses and determine what is helpful from each. Ask participants what language or expectations from the lenses they might be able to use to shape guiding questions for their mentees.

Option 3

Rather than use the examples in the text, you may want to focus on the lens that your district uses. You should have participants review the format of the district evaluation tool to ensure that they are familiar with it and understand its language and expectations. You may wish to have participants consider options for aligning your district's evaluation tool with ideas from one or more of the mentoring lenses listed in the text.

If you do not have a district process for evaluating new teachers, reviewing the various lenses presented in Chapter 5 can help determine which process to use. At the very least, looking at the various lenses gives mentors insight into the kinds of expectations they should have for the development of their mentee.

Question 14: What do I need to know about conferencing skills? (50–70 minutes)

Reading Assignment (10 minutes): Chapter 6, pages 77–79

Dialogue (10 minutes): Preconference Questions, Chapter 6, page 79

Explain that the preconference can help create a more successful observation. Have participants work with a partner to read and evaluate the sample pre-observation questions. Debrief by having participants share with the group the questions they would consider using. If they have other questions they think will help prepare for an observation, they should share those as well.

Reading Assignment (10 minutes): Chapter 6, pages 79–84, The Observation, The Post-Observation Conference

Have participants read about the rest of the conferencing cycle so they can get a sense of the entire process.

Dialogue (10 minutes): The Observation Cycle, Chapter 6, page 81

Ask participants to reread "Dialogue: The Observation Cycle." Tell them that you will model this process for them. Tell them that the goal of this particular dialogue is to put together what they have learned so far and respond to situations that might occur with mentees during an observation cycle.

The situations on pages 82 and 83 give you a list of pre-observation and post-observation situations. Select one and model for your participants how this might be enacted in a role-play. Use a think-aloud process and speak your thoughts so that participants can gain insight into your decisions.

Modeling and Role-Play Activity (30 minutes):

First, choose a lens to use as a basis for gathering information and providing feedback. Tell the group which lens you have chosen and ask them to find the form and review it.

Second, identify which pre-observation situation you have selected. Ask someone to role-play your mentee in this situation. Ask them to try and respond to you as the mentee in the situation might in reality. Read the situation aloud. Now voice your response to the situation, articulating your thoughts and asking the guiding questions of your mentee.

Third, after you feel that you have completed the pre-observation conference, ask the participants what they saw and heard and what they might have been thinking.

Fourth, ask for volunteers to role-play some or all of the situations listed in Figure 6.1. OR ask participants to read through these situations and consider how they would respond. OR assign a particular situation to an individual or group to role-play or analyze and share with the group.

Fifth, select a post-observation conference situation and a different lens and model that for the participants in a fashion similar to what you did with the pre-observation conferences. Repeat the process, with volunteers role-playing some or all of the situations or with participants reading and sharing what they would say and do in such a situation.

Question 15: What are some data-gathering techniques I can use? (50–70 minutes)

Opener: Explain that to provide support for beginning teachers, mentors will need to watch them in action. Opportunities for the two to observe each other and talk about the observations are an absolute necessity for an effective mentorship program. Informal observations are a good way to begin, but how can the mentor shape these observations and discussions to provide more depth to the conversation? Beyond the form on page 45, which was used previously, there are other tools that can help mentors focus their observations and provide a format for feedback. These tools should be used after conversations with mentees, so that both are clear about what will be the focus of the observation.

Reading Assignment (20 minutes): Chapter 7, pages 85–101, Data-Gathering Techniques and Tools

Have participants read this chapter to familiarize themselves with the various data-gathering tools.

Dialogue (10 minutes): Various Scripting Formats, Chapter 7, page 95

Have participants work with a partner to review the various scripting tools in Figures 7.1, 7.2, 7.3, 7.4, 7.5, and 7.6 and determine which tools they are most comfortable using.

Activity (20 minutes): Give participants practice using the scripting formats. Present a video of a classroom situation. (These can be tapes that are filmed in your school or district classroom, or they can be professional teaching tapes that have been purchased.) Have participants watch and script using the scripting format of their choice, then share what information they captured.

Dialogue (10 minutes): Proximity Analysis, Chapter 7, page 97

Direct participants to work with partners to review the proximity analysis on page 97 and consider what the data show. Practice sharing this information with a partner.

Dialogue (10 minutes): Verbal Flow, Chapter 7, page 99

Direct participants to work with partners to review the verbal-flow diagram and consider the data it captured. Then have the partners practice how they would share this data with a mentee.

Dialogue (10 minutes): Use of Numeric Data, Chapter 7, page 101

Consider the questions and share with a partner your views on the use of numeric data.

(Tip to facilitators: Having participants role-play with a partner to practice giving feedback using the various tools will strengthen their skills and enhance your workshop. Mentors can observe and critique each other's skills prior to working with a new teacher. Videotaping these conferences is recommended as tapes provide invaluable feedback for mentors as they learn to use these skills.)

Question 16: Evaluation—What is its role in a mentoring program? (20 minutes)

Reading Assignment (20 minutes): Chapter 8, pages 103–114

Have participants read and review the forms that can be used for evaluation of the effectiveness of those involved in the mentoring relationship.

Activity (20 minutes): Prior to the workshop, review the evaluation forms and identify the ones you will be using in your program. During the workshop, have participants find a partner and discuss the data that such an evaluation will provide and how this will be helpful in facilitating ongoing development for everyone involved.

Activity (15 minutes): Have all participants complete the post-test and have them compare this to their responses on the pre-test. Discuss possible topics for future sessions to continue the learning and support for mentors.

Discussion (20 minutes): Ask participants if they think there is ever a time when the mentor completes a formal evaluation of the mentee. Explain that while the mentor should never be asked to evaluate the mentee for district retention, there are times when a mentor may be asked to provide a letter of recommendation for a mentee who is moving on to another district. In addition, the mentee may ask for such a letter just to have it available for future use. In either case, a mentor needs to be prepared to provide such a document.

Reading Assignment (15 minutes): Chapter 8, pages 114–120, to see guidelines and examples of letters of recommendation.

Dialogue (10 minutes): In pairs, have participants review the letters. Ask them to identify the effect each letter might have and suggest possible statements they would want to use in their future letters of recommendation.

Final Practice Activity: Using the scenarios in Resource B, pages 125–126, have mentors read and think about giving feedback to these mentees. Then have them select and model a post-observation conference with one mentor acting as a student from the post-observation scenarios. Be sure everyone has a chance to respond as the mentor. Videotape the practice sessions and have participants watch the tapes and critique their own efforts based on the skills discussed and practiced in the workshop.

Close by debriefing the practice sessions and answering final questions.

Resource D

Web Sites for Mentors

Best Practices Resources: http://www.teachermentors.com
Provides a wide range of links for mentors on all aspects of teaching

Mentoring Leadership & Resource Network: http://www.mentors.net
Detailed resources and support for mentors as well as discussions of mentoring topics

Mighty Mentors: http://www.teaching.com/mentors
Network that matches novice teachers to veteran teachers for e-mail mentoring

National Board for Professional Standards: http://www.nbpts.org/
Includes information about National Board certification

Teachers Helping Teachers: http://www.pacificnet.net/~mandel/
Links to all topics related to teaching provided by teachers

Mighty Media Resources: http://www.teaching.com
A site for mentors to locate resources and problem-solve about teaching issues

TeacherNet—The Student-Teacher Resource Page: http://www.csulb.edu/~jmcasey/
A way to connect with other teachers to share ideas

Teacher Talk: http://education.indiana.edu/cas/tt/tthmpg.html
For preservice secondary education teachers

Northwest Regional Laboratory: http://www.nwrel.org/
Home page devoted to curricula and lesson plans

Bibliography

Allen, D., Cobb, J., & Danger, S. (2003). Inservice teachers mentoring aspiring teachers. *Mentoring and Tutoring, 11*(2), 177–182.

Barrett, J. (2000). Relationships. In M. Boushel, M. Fawcett, & J. Selwyn (Eds.), *Focus on early childhood.* Oxford, UK: Blackwell Science.

Bartell, C. (2004). *Cultivating high-quality teaching through induction and mentoring.* Thousand Oaks, CA: Corwin Press.

Bey, T. (1992). Mentoring in teacher education: Diversifying support for teachers. In T. Bey & C. Holmes (Eds.), *Mentoring: Contemporary principles and issues* (pp. 111–113). Reston, VA: Association of Teacher Educators.

Blake, S. (1999). At the crossroads of race and gender: Lessons from the mentoring experiences of professional black women. In A. Murrell, F. Crosby, & R. Ely (Eds.), *Mentoring dilemmas: Developing relationships within multicultural organizations* (pp. 83–104). Mahwah, NJ: Lawrence Erlbaum Associates.

Bleach, K. (1999). *The induction and mentoring of newly qualified teachers: A deal for new teachers.* London: David Fulton.

Boreen, J., Johnson, M., Niday, D., & Potts, J. (2000). *Mentoring beginning teachers: Guiding, reflecting, coaching.* New York: Stenhouse.

Bouquillon, E., Sosik, J., & Lee, D. (2005). "It's only a phase": Examining trust, identification and mentoring functions received across the mentoring phases. *Mentoring and Tutoring, 13*(2), 239–258.

Brock, B., & Grady, M. (2005). *Developing a beginning teacher induction plan.* Thousand Oaks, CA: Corwin Press.

Brooks, V. (2000). School-based initial teacher training: Squeezing a quart into a pint pot or a square peg into a round hole? *Mentoring and Tutoring, 8*(2), 99–112.

Brooks, V., Sikes, P., & Husbands, C. (1997). *The good mentor guide: Initial teacher education in secondary schools.* Buckingham, UK: Open University Press.

Brown, J. (1995). *Observing dimensions of learning in classrooms and schools.* Alexandria, VA: Association for Supervision and Curriculum Development.

Butler, T., & Chao, T. (2001). Partners for change: Students as effective technology mentors. *Active Learning in Higher Education, 2*(2), 101–113.

Chapel, S. (2003). Responsibilities of subject mentors, professional mentors and link tutors in secondary physical education initial teacher education. *Mentoring and Tutoring, 11*(2), 131–151.

Chubbuck, S., Clift, R., Allard, J., & Quinlan, J. (2001). Playing it safe as a novice teacher: Implications for programs for new teachers. *Journal of Teacher Education, 52*(5), 365–376.

Cobb, A., Stephens, C., & Watson, G. (2001). Beyond structure: The role of social accounts in implementing ideal control. *Human Relations, 54*(9), 1123–1153.

Council of Chief State School Officers. (1992). *Model standards for beginning teacher licensing, assessment, and development: A resource for state dialogue.* Washington, DC: Author. Retrieved from http://www.ccsso.org/content/pdfs/corestrd.pdf

Cowne, E., & Little, S. (1999). Giving up my kids: Two mentor teachers' stories. In P. Graham, S. Hudson-Ross, C. Adkins, P. McWhorter, & J. Stewart (Eds.), *Teacher/mentor: A dialogue for collaborative learning* (pp. 46–52). New York: Teachers College Press.

Cuddapah, J. (2002). *The teachers college new teacher institute: Supporting new teachers through mentoring relationships.* Paper presented at the annual meeting of the American Educational Research Association. (ERIC Document Reproduction Service No. ED470683)

Danielson, C. (1996). *Enhancing professional practice: A framework for teaching.* Alexandria, VA: Association for Supervision and Curriculum Development.

Danielson, C., & McGreal, T. (2000). *Teacher evaluation to enhance professional practice.* Princeton, NJ: Educational Testing Service.

Daresh, J. (2002). *Teachers mentoring teachers.* Thousand Oaks, CA: Corwin Press.

Darling-Hammond, L. (2003). Keeping good teachers: Why it matters what leaders can do. *Educational Leadership, 60*(8), 6–13.

Delgado, M. (1999). Developing competent practitioners. *Educational Leadership, 56*(8), 45–48.

Dindia, K. (2000). Self disclosure, identity and relationship development: A dialectical perspective. In K. Dindia & S. Duck (Eds.), *Communication and personal relationships.* Chichester, UK: Wiley.

Dindia, K., & Duck, S. (Eds.). (2000). *Communication and personal relationships.* Chichester, UK: Wiley.

Educational Testing Service. (1995). *Teacher performance assessments: A comparative view.* Princeton, NJ: Author.

Ellis, K. (2002). A model class. *Training, 37*(12), 50–57.

Enz, B. (1992). Guidelines for selecting mentors and creating an environment for mentoring. In T. Bey & C. Holmes (Eds.), *Mentoring: Contemporary principles and issues* (pp. 65–67). Reston, VA: Association of Teacher Educators.

Evertson, C., & Smithey, M. (2000). Mentoring effects on protégés' classroom practice: An experimental field study. *Journal of Educational Research, 93*(5), 294–304.

Fabian, H., & Simpson, A. (2002). Mentoring the experienced teacher. *Mentoring and Tutoring, 10*(2), 117–125.

Feiman-Nemser, S. (2001, April). *Combining assistance and formative assessment: The case of the Santa Cruz New Teacher Project.* Paper presented at the annual meeting of the American Educational Research Association, Seattle, WA.

Feiman-Nemser, S. (2003). What new teachers need to learn. *Educational Leadership, 60*(8), 25–29.

Feiman-Nemser, S., Carver, C., Schwille, S., & Yusko, B. (1999). Beyond support: Taking new teachers seriously as learners. In M. Scherer (Ed.), *A better beginning: Supporting and mentoring new teachers* (pp. 3–12). Alexandria, VA: Association for Supervision and Curriculum Development.

Fideler, E., & Haselkorn, D. (1999). *Learning the ropes: Urban teacher induction programs and practices in the United States.* Belmont, MA: Recruiting New Teachers.

Fletcher, S. (2004). Developing effective beginning teachers through mentor-based induction. *Mentoring and Tutoring, 12*(3), 321–333.

Furlong, J., & Maynard, T. (1995). *Mentoring student teachers: The growth of professional knowledge.* New York: Routledge.

Ganser, T. (1996). What do mentors say about mentoring? *Journal of Staff Development, 17*(3), 62–69.

Garvey, B. (1999). Mentoring and the changing paradigm. *Mentoring and Tutoring, 7*(1), 41–54.

Garvey, B., & Alred, G. (2000). Educating mentors. *Mentoring and Tutoring, 8*(2), 113–126.

Garza, L., & Wurzbach, L. (2002). Texas plan drowns the idea of sink-or-swim induction. *Journal of Staff Development, 12*(4), 41–45.

Geen, A., Bassett, P., & Douglas, L. (1999). The role of the secondary school subject mentor: An evaluation of the UWIC experience. *Mentoring and Tutoring, 7*(1), 55–65.

Giebelhaus, C., & Bowman, C. (2000). *Teaching mentors: Is it worth the effort?* Paper presented at the Annual Meeting of the Association of Teacher Educators, Orlando, FL. (ERIC Document Reproduction Service No. ED438277)

Gilbert, L. (2005). What helps beginning teachers? *Educational Leadership, 62*(8), 36–39.

Gilles, C., Cramer, M., & Hwang-Lee, S. (2001). New teacher perceptions of concerns: A longitudinal look at teacher development. *Action in Teacher Education, 23*(3), 92–96.

Gilles, C., & Wilson, J. (2004). Receiving as well as giving: Mentors' perceptions of their professional development in one teacher induction program. *Mentoring and Teaching, 12*(1), 87–106.

Glickman, C., Gordon, S., & Ross-Gordon, J. (1997). *Supervision of instruction: A developmental approach* (4th ed.). Boston: Allyn & Bacon.

Gold, Y. (1992). Psychological support for mentors and beginning teachers: A critical dimension. In T. Bey & C. Holmes (Eds.), *Mentoring: Contemporary principles and issues* (pp. 25–34). Reston, VA: Association of Teacher Educators.

Gold, Y. (1999). Beginning teacher support: Attrition, mentoring, and induction. In J. Sikula, T. Buttery, & E. Guyton (Eds.), *Handbook of research on teacher education* (2nd ed., pp. 548–594). New York: Macmillan.

Graham, P. (1998). *A dialogue for collaborative learning.* New York: Teachers College Press.

Graham, P., Hudson-Ross, S., Adkins, C., McWhorter, P., & Stewart, J. (Eds.). (1999). *Teacher/mentor: A dialogue for collaborative learning.* New York: Teachers College Press.

Hayes, D. (1999). A matter of being willing? Mentors' expectations of student primary teachers. *Mentoring and Tutoring, 7*(1), 67–79.

Head, F., Reiman, A., & Theis-Sprinthall, L. (1992). The reality of mentoring: Complexity in its process and function. In T. Bey & C. Holmes (Eds.), *Mentoring: Contemporary principles and issues* (pp. 5–24). Reston, VA: Association of Teacher Educators.

Hicks, C., Glasgow, N., & McNary, S. (2004). *What successful mentors do.* Thousand Oaks, CA: Corwin Press.

Hobson, A. (2002). Student teachers' perception of school-based mentoring in initial teacher training (ITT). *Mentoring and Tutoring, 10*(2), 5–20.

Holloway, J. (2001). The benefits of mentoring. *Educational Leadership, 58*(8), 57–67.

Huling-Austin, L. (1990). Mentoring is squishy business. In T. Bey & C. Holmes (Eds.), *Mentoring: Developing successful new teachers* (pp. 39–50). Reston, VA: Association of Teacher Educators.

Ingersoll, R., & Kralik, J. (2004). *The impact of mentoring on teacher retention: What the research says.* Denver, CO: Education Commission of the States.

John, P., & Gilchrist, I. (1999). Flying solo: Understanding the post-lesson dialogue between student teacher and mentor. *Mentoring and Tutoring, 7*(2), 101–111.

Johnson, D., & Johnson, F. (2002). *Joining together* (8th ed.). Boston: Allyn & Bacon.

Johnson, K. (2002). *How to help beginning teachers succeed.* Thousand Oaks, CA: Corwin Press.

Johnson, S., Berg, J., & Donaldson, M. (2003). *Who stays in teaching and why: A review of the literature on teacher retention.* Boston: Harvard Graduate School of Education.

Johnson, S., & The Project on the Next Generation of Teachers. (2004). *Finders keepers: Helping new teachers survive and thrive in schools.* San Francisco: Jossey-Bass.

Johnson-Bailey, J., & Cervero, R. (2004). Mentoring in black and white: The intricacies of cross-cultural mentoring. *Mentoring and Tutoring, 12*(1), 7–21.

Kay, R. (1989). Evaluation of beginning teacher assistance programs. In L. Huling-Austin, S. Odell, P. Ishler, R. Kay, & R. Edelfelt (Eds.), *Assisting the beginning teacher.* Reston, VA: Association of Teacher Educators.

Kay, R. (1990). A definition for developing self-reliance. In T. Bey & C. Holmes (Eds.), *Mentoring: Developing successful new teachers.* Reston, VA: Association of Teacher Educators.

Kay, R. (1992). Mentor-management: Emphasizing the HUMAN in managing human resources. In T. Bey & C. Holmes (Eds.), *Mentoring: Contemporary principles and issues* (pp. 51–63). Reston, VA: Association of Teacher Educators.

Kelchtermans, G., & Ballet, K. (2003). The micropolitics of teacher induction: A narrative-biological study on teacher socialization. *Teaching and Teacher Education, 18*(1), 105–120.

Larsson, R., & Lubatkin, M. (2001). Achieving acculturation in mergers and acquisitions: An international case survey. *Human Relations, 54*(12), 1573–1607.

Latham, A., Gitomer, D., & Ziomek, R. (1999). What the tests tell us about new teachers. *Educational Leadership, 56*(8), 23–26.

Lieberman, A., & Miller, L. (1984). *Teachers, their world and their work.* Reston, VA: Association for Supervision and Curriculum Development.

Lindley, F. (2003). *The portable mentor.* Thousand Oaks, CA: Corwin Press.

Lipton, L., Wellman, B., & Humbard, C. (2003). *Mentoring matters: A practical guide to learning-focused relationships* (2nd ed.). Sherman, CT: Mira Via.

Little, J. (1990). The mentor phenomenon. In C. B. Cazden (Ed.), *Review of Research in Education* (Vol. 16, pp. 297–351). Washington, DC: American Educational Research Association.

Little, P. (2005). Peer coaching as a support to collaborative teaching. *Mentoring and Tutoring, 13*(1), 83–94.

Lucas, C. (1999). Lifesaving 101: How a veteran teacher can help a beginner. *Educational Leadership, 56*(8), 27–29.

Maldevez, A., & Bodoczky, C. (1999). *Mentor courses: A resource book for teacher-trainers.* New York: Cambridge University Press.

Manusov, V. (2005). *The sourcebook of nonverbal measures: Going beyond words.* Mahwah, NJ: Erlbaum.

Marshall, H. (1990). Metaphor as an instructional tool in encouraging student teacher reflection. *Theory Into Practice, 29*(2), 128–132.

Marzano, R., Pickering, D., Arredondo, D., Blackburn, G., Brandt, R., & Moffett, C. (1992). *Dimensions of learning teacher's manual.* Reston, VA: Association for Supervision and Curriculum Development.

Maynard, T. (2000). Learning to teach or learning to manage mentors? Experiences of school-based teacher training. *Mentoring and Tutoring, 8*(1), 17–30.

McCann, T., Johannessen, L., & Ricca, B. (2005). Responding to new teachers' concerns. *Educational Leadership, 62*(8), 30–34.

Metts, S. (2000). Face and facework: Implications for the study of personal relationships. In K. Dindia & S. Duck (Eds.), *Communication and personal relationships* (pp. 77–93). Chichester, UK: Wiley.

Moir, E., & Bloom, G. (2003). Fostering leadership through mentoring. *Educational Leadership, 60*(8), 58–60.

Moir, E., Gless, J., & Baron, W. (1999). A support program with heart: The Santa Cruz project. In M. Scherer (Ed.), *A better beginning: Supporting and mentoring new teachers* (pp. 106–115). Alexandria, VA: Association for Supervision and Curriculum Development.

Moir, E., & Stobbe, C. (1995). Professional growth for new teachers: Supports and assessment through collegial partnerships. *Teacher Education Quarterly, 22*(4), 83–91.

Mullen, C. (2000). Post-sharkdom: An alternate form of mentoring for teacher educators.

Mullen, C. (2002). Web-enhanced instruction: A mixed bag of contradictions and possibilities for doctoral education. *Online Journal of Academic Leadership, 2*(2), 1–37.

Mullen, C., Cox, M., Boettcher, C., & Adoue, D. (Eds.). (2000). *Breaking the circle of one: Redefining mentorships in the lives and writings of educators* (2nd ed, pp. 145–174) New York: Peter Lang.

Mutchler, S. (2000). Lessons from research on teacher mentoring: Review of the literature. *Mentoring beginning teachers: Lessons from the experience in Texas.* Austin, TX: Southwest Educational Development Laboratory.

National Center for Education Statistics. (1999). *Teacher quality: A report on the preparation and qualifications of public school teachers* (NCES Report No. 19999080). Washington, DC: Authors.

National Commission on Teaching and America's Future. (2000). *NCRTL explores learning from mentors: A study update.* Retrieved July 29, 2005, from http://www.educ.msu.edu/alumni/newed/ne66c3~5.htm

Neal, J. (1992). Mentoring: A teacher development activity that avoids formal evaluation of the protégé. In T. Bey & C. Holmes (Eds.), *Mentoring: Contemporary principles and issues* (pp. 35–50). Reston, VA: Association of Teacher Educators.

Obidah, J., & Teel, K. (2001). *Because of the kids: Facing racial and cultural differences in schools.* New York: Teachers College Press.

Odell, S. (1992). Evaluating mentoring programs. In T. Bey & C. Holmes (Eds.), *Mentoring: Contemporary principles and issues* (pp. 95–101). Reston, VA: Association of Teacher Educators.

Odell, S., & Huling, L. (2000). *Quality mentoring for novice teachers.* Indianapolis, IN: Kappa Delta Pi.

Olebe, M., Jackson, A., & Danielson, C. (1999). Investing in beginning teachers: The California model. *Educational Leadership, 56*(8), 41–44.

Orland, L. (2000). Reading a mentoring situation: One aspect of learning to mentor. *Teaching and Teacher Education, 17*(1), 75–88.

Orland-Barak, L. (2005). Lost in translation: Mentors learning to participate in competing discourses of practice. *Journal of Teacher Education, 56*(4), 355–366.

Peterson, B. (2004). *Cultural intelligence: A guide to working with people from other cultures.* Yarmouth, ME: Intercultural Press.

Pitton, D. (1994). Mentoring: The special needs of student teachers. *People and Education, 2*(3), 338–352.

Pitton, D. (1998). *Stories of student teaching: A case approach to the student teaching experience.* Upper Saddle River, NJ: Merrill/Prentice-Hall.

Podsen, I., & Denmark, V. (2000). *Coaching and mentoring first-year and student teachers.* Larchmont, NY: Eye on Education.

Portner, H. (2003). *Mentoring new teachers.* Thousand Oaks, CA: Corwin Press.

Portner, H. (Ed.). (2005). *Teacher mentoring and induction.* Thousand Oaks, CA: Corwin Press.

Reiman, A., & Edefelt, R. (1990). *School-based mentoring programs: Untangling the tensions between theory and practice* (Research report 90–7). Chapel Hill: University of North Carolina, Department of Curriculum and Instruction.

Reiman, A., Head, F., & Theis-Sprinthall, L. (1992). Collaboration and mentoring. In T. Bey & C. Holmes (Eds.), *Mentoring: Contemporary principles and issues* (pp. 79–93). Reston, VA: Association of Teacher Educators.

Renard, L. (2003). Setting new teachers up for failure . . . or success. *Educational Leadership, 60*(8), 62–64.

Rippon, J., & Martin, M. (2002). Supporting induction: Relationships count. *Mentoring and Tutoring, 11*(2), 211–226.

Roberts, A. (2000). Mentoring revisited: A phenomenological reading of the literature. *Mentoring and Tutoring, 8*(2), 145–170.

Rosenfeld, L. B. (1979). Self-disclosure avoidance: Why I am afraid to tell you who I am. *Communication Monographs, 46,* 72–73.

Rowley, J. (1999). The good mentor. *Educational Leadership, 56*(8), 20–22.

Rudney, G., & Guillame, A. (2003). *Maximum mentoring.* Thousand Oaks, CA: Corwin Press.

Saurino, D., & Saurino, P. (1999). *Making effective use of mentoring teacher programs: A collaborative group action research approach.* Paper presented at the annual meeting of the National Association for Research in Science Teaching. (ERIC Document Reproduction Service No. ED429963)

Schon, D. (1990). *Educating the reflective practitioner.* San Francisco: Jossey-Bass.

Schubert, W., & Ayers, W. (1992). *Teacher lore: Learning from our own experience.* New York: Longman.

Shank, M. (2005). Mentoring among high school teachers: A dynamic and reciprocal group process. *Mentoring and Tutoring, 13*(1), 73–82.

Shea, G. (1998). *Mentoring: How to develop successful mentor behaviors.* Menlo Park, CA: Crisp.

Shulman, J., & Colbert, J. (Eds.). (1988). *The intern teacher casebook.* San Francisco: Far West Laboratory for Education Research.

Sinclair, C. (2003). Mentoring online about mentoring: Possibilities and practice. *Mentoring and Tutoring, 11*(1), 79–95.

Smith, J. (2005). Understanding the beliefs, concerns and priorities of trainee teachers: A multi-disciplinary approach. *Mentoring and Tutoring, 13*(2), 205–219.

Smith, J., & Ingersoll, R. (2004). Reducing teacher turnover: What are the components of effective induction? *American Educational Research Journal, 41*(2), 681–714.

Smith, P. (2001). Mentors as gate-keepers: An exploration of professional formation. *Educational Review, 53*(3), 313–324.

Spindler, J., & Biott, C. (2000). Target setting in the induction of newly qualified teachers: Emerging colleagueship in a context of performance management. *Educational Research, 42*(3), 275–285.

Stansbury, K., & Zimmerman, J. (2000). *Lifelines to the classroom: Designing support for beginning teachers.* San Francisco: WestEd.

Stanulis, R., Fallona, C., & Pearson, C. (2002). Am I doing what I am supposed to be doing? Mentoring novice teachers through the uncertainties and challenges of their first year of teaching. *Mentoring and Tutoring, 10*(1), 71–81.

Storms, B., Wing, J., Jinks, T., Banks, W., & Cavazos, P. (2000). *CFASST (field review) implementation 1999–2000: A formative evaluation report.* Princeton, NJ: Educational Testing Service.

Tannehill, D. (1989). Student teaching: A view from the other side. *Journal of Teaching in Physical Education, 8,* 243–253.

Tatum, B., McWhorter, P., Healan, C., Rhoades, M., Chandler, L., Michael, M., et al. (1999). Maybe not everything, but a whole lot you always wanted to know about mentoring. In P. Graham, S. Hudson-Ross,

C. Adkins, P. McWhorter, & J. Stewart (Eds.), *Teacher/mentor: A dialogue for collaborative learning* (pp. 21–34). New York: Teachers College Press.

Theis-Sprinthall, L., & Reiman, A. (1997). *Mentoring and supervision for teacher development.* Reading, MA: Addison-Wesley.

Thomas, D. (2001). The truth about mentoring minorities: Race matters. *Harvard Business Review, 79*(4), 98–107.

Tinning, R. (1996). Mentoring in the Australian physical education teacher context: Lessons from cooking turkeys and tandoori chicken. In M. Mawer (Ed.), *Mentoring in physical education: Issues and insights* (pp. 197–216). London: Falmer.

Trager, G. (1958). Paralanguage: A first approximation. *Studies in Linguistics, 13*, 1–12.

U.S. Department of Education. (1999). Unpublished tabulations for the 1993–1994 schools and staffing summary and the 1994–1995 teacher follow-up survey. Washington, DC: National Center for Educational Statistics.

Varah, L., Theune, W., & Parker, L. (1986). Beginning teachers: Sink or swim? *Journal of Teacher Education, 37*(1), 30–34.

Villani, S. (2002). *Mentoring programs for new teachers.* Thousand Oaks, CA: Corwin Press.

Wallace, J. (1999). The dialogue journal. In P. Graham, S. Hudson-Ross, C. Adkins, P. McWhorter, & J. Stewart (Eds.), *Teacher/mentor: A dialogue for collaborative learning.* New York: Teachers College Press.

Wayne, A., Young, P., & Fleischman, S. (2005). Improving teacher induction. *Educational Leadership, 62*(8), 76–78.

Wentz, P., & Yarling, J. (1994). *Student teaching casebook for supervising teachers and teaching interns.* Upper Saddle River, NJ: Merrill/Prentice-Hall.

Wolfe, D. (1992). Designing training and selecting incentives for mentor programs. In T. Bey & C. Holmes (Eds.), *Mentoring: Contemporary principles and issues* (pp. 103–109). Reston, VA: Association of Teacher Educators.

Wong, H., & Wong, R. (1998). *The first days of school: How to be an effective teacher.* Mountain View, CA: Harry K. Wong Publications.

Young, J., Alvermann D., Kaste, J., Henderson, S., & Many, J. (2004). Being a friend and a mentor at the same time: A pooled case comparison. *Mentoring and Tutoring, 12*(1), 24–36.

Young, J., Bullough, R., Draper, R., Smith, L., & Erickson, L. (2005). Novice teacher growth and personal models of mentoring: Choosing compassion over inquiry. *Mentoring and Tutoring, 13*(2), 169–188.

Index

**CORWIN
PRESS**

The Corwin Press logo—a raven striding across an open book—represents the union of courage and learning. Corwin Press is committed to improving education for all learners by publishing books and other professional development resources for those serving the field of PreK–12 education. By providing practical, hands-on materials, Corwin Press continues to carry out the promise of its motto: **"Helping Educators Do Their Work Better."**